W9-BEV-924

Bloom's
GUIDES

Toni Morrison's
The Bluest Eye

The Adventures of Huckleberry Finn

All the Pretty Horses

Animal Farm

The Autobiography of Malcolm X

The Awakening

The Bell Jar

Beloved

Beowulf

Black Boy

The Bluest Eye

Brave New World

The Canterbury Tales

Catch-22

The Catcher in the Rye

The Chosen

The Crucible

Cry, the Beloved Country

Death of a Salesman

Fahrenheit 451

A Farewell to Arms

Frankenstein

The Glass Menagerie

The Grapes of Wrath

Great Expectations

The Great Gatsby

Hamlet

The Handmaid's Tale

Heart of Darkness

The House on Mango Street

I Know Why the Caged Bird Sings

The Iliad

Invisible Man

Jane Eyre

The Joy Luck Club

The Kite Runner

Lord of the Flies

Macbeth

Maggie: A Girl of the Streets

The Member of the Wedding

The Metamorphosis

Native Son

Night

1984

The Odyssey

Oedipus Rex

Of Mice and Men

One Hundred Years of Solitude

Pride and Prejudice

Ragtime

A Raisin in the Sun

The Red Badge of Courage

Romeo and Juliet

The Scarlet Letter

A Separate Peace

Slaughterhouse-Five

Snow Falling on Cedars

The Stranger

A Streetcar Named Desire

The Sun Also Rises

A Tale of Two Cities

Their Eyes Were Watching God

The Things They Carried

To Kill a Mockingbird

Uncle Tom's Cabin

The Waste Land

Wuthering Heights

Bloom's
GUIDES

Toni Morrison's
The Bluest Eye

Edited & with an Introduction
by Harold Bloom

BLOOM'S
LITERARY CRITICISM
An imprint of Infobase Publishing

Bloom's Guides: The Bluest Eye

Copyright © 2010 by Infobase Publishing

Introduction © 2010 by Harold Bloom

Bloom's Literary Criticism
An imprint of Infobase Publishing
132 West 31st Street
New York, NY 10001

Library of Congress Cataloging-in-Publication Data
Toni Morrison's The bluest eye / edited and with an introduction by Harold Bloom.
    p. cm. — (Bloom's guides)
Includes bibliographical references and index.
ISBN 978-1-60413-573-2 (hardcover)
1. Morrison, Toni. Bluest eye. 2. African Americans in literature.
3. Girls in literature. I. Bloom, Harold. II. Title. III. Series.
PS3563.O8749B556 2009
813'.54—dc22   2009025685

Contributing Editor: Portia Weiskel
Cover design by Takeshi Takahashi
Printed in the United States of America
IBT IBT 10 9 8 7 6 5 4 3 2 1
This book is printed on acid-free paper.

Contents

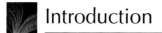 Introduction

HAROLD BLOOM

The Bluest Eye, Toni Morrison's first novel, was published when she was thirty-nine and is anything but a novice work. Michael Wood, an authentic literary critic, made the best comment on this "lucid and eloquent" narrative that I have ever seen:

> Each member of the family interprets and acts out of his or her ugliness, but none of them understands that the all-knowing master is not God but only history and habit; the projection of their own numbed collusion with the mythology of beauty and ugliness that oppresses them beyond their already grim social oppression.

Morrison herself, in an afterword of 1994, looked back across a quarter century and emphasize her "reliance for full comprehension in codes embedded in black culture." A reader who is not black or female must do the best he can; like Michael Wood, I have found *The Bluest Eye* to be completely lucid since I first read it back in 1970. Like *Sula* and *Song of Solomon* after it, the book seems to me successful in universal terms, even if one shares neither Morrison's origins nor her ideologies. *Beloved,* Morrison's most famous romantic narrative, seems to be problematic, though it has reached a vast audience. A generation or two will have to pass before a balanced judgment could be rendered on *Beloved* and Morrison's later novels. But her early phase has many of the canonical qualifications of the traditional Western literary kind that she fiercely rejects as being irrelevant to her.

What I forget about *The Bluest Eye* is its terrifying penultimate paragraph, where the narrator censures herself and her friends for turning away from Pecola because the child's madness, engendered by the trauma of being raped by her father, Cholly, "bored us in the end":

Oh, some of us "loved" her. The Maginot Line. And Cholly loved her. I'm sure he did. He, at any rate, was the one who loved her enough to touch her, envelop her, give something of himself to her. But his touch was fatal, and the something he gave her filled the matrix of her agony and death. Love is never any better than the lover. Wicked people love wickedly, violent people love violently, weak people love weakly, stupid people love stupidly, but the love of a free man is never safe. These is no gift for the beloved. The lover alone possesses his gift of love. The loved one is shorn, neutralized, frozen in the glare of the lover's inward eye.

The unhappy wisdom of this is happily free of any cultural narcissism whatsoever. Class, race, even gender do not overdetermine this bleakness. Morrison's heroic survivors in *Beloved* are intended to stand up both in and against their history. Perhaps they do, but the torments they have endured also are tendentiously elaborated, because the author has an ideological design on us, her guilty readers, black and white, male and female. The narrator of *The Bluest Eye* persuades me, where the narrator of *Beloved* does not. In D.H. Lawrence's terms, I trust both the tale and the teller in *The Bluest Eye*. In *Beloved*, I do not trust the tale.

Biographical Sketch

Raised in the North, Toni Morrison's southern roots were deliberately severed by both her maternal and paternal grandparents. Her maternal grandfather, John Solomon Willis, had his inherited Alabama farm swindled from him by a predatory white man; as a consequence of this injustice, he moved his family first to Kentucky, where a less overt racism continued to make life intolerable, and then to Lorain, Ohio, a midwestern industrial center with employment possibilities that were drawing large numbers of migrating southern blacks. Her paternal grandparents also left their Georgia home in reaction to the hostile, racist culture that included lynchings and other oppressive acts. As a result, the South as a region did not exist as a benevolent inherited resource for Morrison while she was growing up; it became more of an estranged section of the country from which she had been helped to flee. As is evident in her novels, Morrison returned by a spiritually circuitous route to the strong southern traditions that would again be reinvigorated and re-experienced as life sustaining.

The future Nobel literature laureate was born Chloe Ardelia Wofford at home in Lorain, Ohio, on February 18, 1931, the second child and daughter to George and Ella Ramah Willis Wofford. Two distinguishing experiences in her early years were, first, living with the sharply divided views of her parents about race (her father was actively disdainful of white people, her mother more focused on individual attitudes and behavior) and, second, beginning elementary school as the only child already able to read.

This latter distinction was a result of her family's stress on acquiring cultural literacy, especially in literature and music. Her maternal grandfather was an accomplished violinist, and her mother was a talented singer who performed in the church choir and sang frequently around the house. Folk music was especially prominent. Reading and storytelling were also promoted. Both parents liked to tell stories from their respective family histories and also invented ghost stories their children recalled as fun but genuinely scary. Morrison was such an advanced reader that she was asked to tutor others in her class, and she spent much of her nonschool time in the Lorain Public Library—so happily and productively, in fact, that years later, on January 22, 1995, the Lorain Public Library dedicated the new Toni Morrison Reading Room at a public ceremony that she attended. With such ability and support, Morrison was able to excel at school. Years later, she recalled having been profoundly drawn to the classical writers—Austen, Flaubert, Dostoevsky, and others. She said she knew these books "were not written for a little black girl in Lorain, Ohio, but they were so magnificently done that I got them anyway—they spoke directly to me out of their own specificity" (Jean Strouse, "Toni Morrison's Black Magic," *Newsweek*, March 30, 1981 [53–54]).

Although racial issues did not dominate family discussions, Morrison did observe her mother resisting the northern (more subtle) brand of discrimination practiced in Lorain, Ohio (and the North, in general), when she carried out a small act of rebellion by refusing to sit in the section of the local movie theater set aside for blacks. Racial issues were being confronted across the United States at the time and this fact, coupled with her father's active disdain for white people, ensured that Toni Morrison grew up with a "politicizing" awareness.

Morrison became the first person from either side of her family to attend college. She entered Howard University in 1949 and graduated with honors in 1953 after studying literature, the classics, and art. The poet Amiri Baraka (Leroi Jones) was one of her classmates. It was while she was at Howard that she changed her original name to Toni, for reasons never fully disclosed.

After Howard, Morrison studied at Cornell, earning her master's degree with a thesis comparing alienation and suicide in the writings of William Faulkner and Virginia Woolf; after her graduate studies, she took a job teaching literature at Texas Southern University. By then, it was evident that Morrison was headed for a career teaching literature at the college level. She returned to Howard after two years and remained there as an instructor between 1957 and 1965. Among the students she taught there were three who would go on to take prominent roles in the civil rights and Black Power movements—Andrew Young, Claude Brown, and Stokely Carmichael.

Morrison was married during this period to a Jamaican-born architect, Harold Morrison. The couple had two sons, divorcing in 1964 while Morrison was pregnant with the second child. She went back briefly to Lorain to live with her family before relocating to Syracuse, New York, where she took a job as a textbook editor for a division of Random House. It was an important role that she assumed in this job: being responsible for helping to change the way black people were represented in school curricula. In 1967, Morrison was promoted to senior editor, and she moved to New York to take the position.

It was during this difficult time of overwork and isolation that Morrison joined a fiction and poetry writing group and began writing during the infrequent parts of the day when she was not working and when her children were sleeping. The story she was working on became her first novel, *The Bluest Eye*, but it took years to get the attention required to become a publishable work. Of this early effort at writing—which no one, certainly not Morrison herself, knew would initiate a new and significant career for her—she recalled how little time she had for this new effort and said, "I wrote like someone with a dirty habit. Secretly, compulsively, and slyly" (quoted in Karen Carmean, *Toni Morrison's World of Fiction*, 1993, 4). The manuscript was turned down by several publishers before Holt, Rinehart, and Winston published it in 1970 with the title of *The Bluest Eye*. Although the novel was not a commercial success, its appearance marked the beginning of the career Toni Morrison could from then on never imagine herself not pursuing.

Achievements, accolades, and opportunities began to escalate for Toni Morrison after the publication of *Sula* in 1973. The novel was nominated for a National Book Award (1975); she took a position as a faculty member at the Bread Loaf Writer's Conference in Vermont; she was offered and accepted a visiting lectureship at Yale; *Song of Solomon* came out in 1977 for which Morrison won the National Book Critics' Circle Award and the

American Academy and Institute of Arts and Letters Award. Finally financially independent, Morrison was able to purchase a home on the Hudson River in New York. In 1980, Morrison was appointed to the National Council on the Arts by President Jimmy Carter, and a year later she was doubly honored with membership in the American Academy of Arts and Sciences and a cover story in *Newsweek* magazine.

In 1987, Morrison's fifth novel, *Beloved*, was published; it became a Book-of-the-Month Club selection but was not named a finalist for the National Book Award, an omission felt so keenly that, a year later, a group of almost 50 African-American writers published a statement of protest in the *New York Times Book Review*. Later that year, Morrison won the Pulitzer Prize for fiction, and one year later, in 1989, she became the first African-American woman to hold an endowed university chair when she was appointed the Robert E. Goheen Professor in the Council of Humanities at Princeton University. While at Princeton, she established the Atelier program, which brought to the university artists of all kinds to work directly with students on their projects and productions. It was also during this time that her sixth novel, *Jazz*, was released and, most notably, she became the first African-American woman to win the Nobel Prize in literature. Since receiving the award in 1993, she has produced three novels, *Paradise, Love*, and *A Mercy*.

Toni Morrison began her writing career and appearance in the mainstream culture in the 1960s—the civil rights/anti–Vietnam War decade characterized by contentious public conversation about the value and role of art versus the value and role of politics. Ralph Ellison had earlier made a major statement asserting the right of the novelist to be or not to be explicitly political while at the same time acknowledging that the novelist will inescapably be political if writing about people and their circumstances. The important point was to make clear that imaginative fictional writing at its best was always about something beside or beyond politics. Morrison concurred with this view. In any of a dozen interviews (see *Conversations with Toni Morrison*, Taylor-Guthrie, 1994), she stated her intention to write in the storytelling tradition of her African forebears who passed on the legends, achievements, and wisdom of one generation to the next. She also asserted her conviction to create characters with stories capable of pulling readers out of their comfortable assurances and assumptions, stating that "the best art is political" and can be "unquestionably political and irrevocably beautiful at the same time" ("Rootedness: The Ancestor as Foundation," *Black Women Writers (1950–1980)*, 3). The special term Morrison uses for this feature of her writing is "bearing witness"—the artist's task of raising awareness and interpreting the past to create coherence and harmony among peoples in the present.

Morrison has engaged in many high-profile political issues. In 1986, she tapped her interest in theater to write a play called *Dreaming Emmett* about the shocking and unsolved murder of Emmett Till and then produced it onstage in Albany, New York. She also published a book of essays on the contentious hearings for Clarence Thomas's nomination to the Supreme Court, *Race-Ing Justice, Engendering Power: Essays on Anita Hill, Clarence Thomas and the Construction of Social Reality* (1992). As a sign of her engagement with the Black Power movement, she edited and published the writings of Huey P. Newton, titled *To Die for the People: The Writings of Huey P. Newton* (1995). Two years after the controversial O.J. Simpson murder trial, Morrison co-edited *Birth of a Nation 'hood: Gaze, Script, and Spectacle in the O.J. Simpson Case* (1997).

Less known about Morrison is her musical ability; in this area, too, she has used her talent to tell important stories with profound political consequences. She based her novel *Beloved* (1987) on the story of Margaret Garner, the historical figure who escaped from slavery in Kentucky and fled to Ohio with her two children, where, when recaptured, she chose to kill both (and succeeded with one) rather than see them returned to slavery. Wanting a context to express the larger-than-life emotions contained in this woman's story and the sensational trial that followed, Morrison wrote a libretto for an opera, *Margaret Garner*, with music by Richard Danielpour. It was first performed in Detroit, Cincinnati, and Philadelphia in

2005–2006, and in September 2007 it was the season opener for the New York City Opera.

A writer who has never shied away from confronting the harsh realities that undergird and influence individual and collective history, Morrison credits the women in her family for encouraging a resolve to write about what others have too easily dismissed as the "unspeakable." These relatives and forbears displayed a capacity for

almost infinite love . . . [and] a clarity about who [they were]. . . . They [had] this . . . intimate relationship with God and death and all sorts of things that strike fear into the modern heart. . . . They never knew from one day to the next about anything, but they . . . believed they were people of value, and they had to pass that on. . . . [One] of the interesting things about feminine intelligence is that it can look at the world as though we can do two . . . or three things at once. . . . [W]e're managing households and other people's children and two jobs and listening to everybody and at the same time creating, singing, holding, bearing, transferring the culture for generations. We've been walking on water for four hundred years. ("A Conversation with Toni Morrison," *Conversations with Toni Morrison*, 269–270)

The Story Behind the Story

In 1980, poet Gwendolyn Brooks published the following poem/love letter she had written for her black female compatriots:

> You have not bought Blondine.
> You have not hailed the hot-comb recently.
> You never worshipped Marilyn Monroe.
> You say: Farrah's hair is hers.
> You have not wanted to be white.
> ....
> The natural respect of Self and Seal!
>   Sisters!
> Your hair is Celebration in the world!

Toni Morrison's novel *The Bluest Eye* and Gwendolyn Brooks's poem are two manifestations of the same cultural phenomenon. Brooks called her poem/love letter "To Those of My Sisters Who Kept Their Naturals" and wrote it to praise and encourage the resistance by black people to white ideology and standards of appearance and conduct, especially the notion of beauty as it was ubiquitously promoted throughout American culture in advertising, television and film, beauty contests, and—until the 1970s—the Dick and Jane reader that was widely used in elementary schools across the United States. The little girl, Pecola Breedlove, in Morrison's *The Bluest Eye*, suffers to the point of self-extinction because of this cultural blindness and lack of all-inclusive representations.

Brooks's poem is addressed to the pioneers of the "Black Is Beautiful" movement who had lived through and were finally emerging from the turbulent years just before, after, and during the decade of the 1960s. The effort to establish unfettered voting rights for black people in the United States did not begin with full resolve until the late 1950s when voter registration drives were organized by black and white citizens, mainly students, many from the North, who traveled in groups to targeted sites in the southern states. The 1960s began with an escalation of these efforts, which merged with the antiwar and antiestablishment movements. These initiatives were at first predominantly nonviolent but, because of backlash and frustration, became, in a few instances, increasingly militant and overtly angry. By the end of the decade the Black Power movement of Malcolm X and the "Black Is Beautiful" declaration had acquired formidable strength and emotional staying power.

This was the decade in which Toni Morrison was beginning to focus on her writing, publishing *The Bluest Eye* in 1970. In addition to the aforementioned developments of this period that form the political and social background for reading *The Bluest Eye* were the efforts by the freedom riders to challenge segregation laws in the Deep South (1961); the civil rights march on Washington, D.C. led by Martin Luther King Jr. (1963); the adoption of the Twenty-fourth Amendment that eliminated the poll tax in federal elections (1964); the passage of the Civil Rights Act (1964); the Watts riots in Los Angeles and the assassination of Malcolm X (1965); the march on Selma, Alabama, led by King (1965); racial rioting in Newark, New Jersey, and Detroit (1967); the assassinations of King and Robert F. Kennedy (1968); and the murders of two prominent leaders of the black separatist movement by the FBI (1969). Another development relevant to the novel, set in motion by the women's rights movement, was the beginning of public acknowledgement and discussion of rape as a social issue. Feminists staged consciousness-raising protests, the first rape crisis center was established in Berkeley, California, and black women writers began writing about rape and incest from the period of slavery to the present.

Morrison was, of course, familiar with the mantra "Black Is Beautiful" and the resistance to established standards of beauty it expressed, but she had no illusions about how deeply in the black psyche the opposite message had been embedded and how much effort and understanding would be required to bring about an enduring reversal in attitude. In a 1980 interview with Kathy Neustadt, Morrison said

[N]obody was going to tell me that it had been that easy. That all I needed was a slogan: 'Black is Beautiful.' It wasn't that easy. Being a little Black girl in this country— it was rough. The psychological tricks you have to play in order to get through—and nobody said how it felt to be that. (Originally published in the *Bryn Mawr Alumnae Bulletin* of Spring 1980 and quoted in *African American Literature and the Classicist Tradition* 2007, 131)

As a writer, Toni Morrison has been open and generous in sharing what her intentions are for writing as she does and in providing insight about what she hopes the effect will be on readers. In a 1981 conversation with Charles Ruas, for example, Morrison explained the original source for *The Bluest Eye*. It began as a short story based on a conversation Morrison had had with a friend during her childhood. Both little girls were discussing the existence of God; Morrison believed, her little friend did not. The reason given for this absence of belief was the absence of a response from God to a prayer the little girl had been submitting every night asking for the "privilege" of having blue eyes. Morrison later reflected:

I looked at her and imagined her having them [blue eyes] and thought how awful that would be if she had gotten her prayer answered. I always thought she was beautiful. I began to write about a girl who wanted blue eyes and the horror of having that wish fulfilled; and also about the whole business of what is physical beauty and the pain of that yearning and wanting to be somebody else, and how devastating that was and yet part of all females who were peripheral in other people's lives. (*Conversations with Toni Morrison*, 1994, 95–96)

Morrison was also forthcoming about her personal motivations for writing. Candidly, she has indicated she would have preferred reading to writing, but in an interview with Claudia Tate in 1983 she acknowledged, "I wrote *Sula* [her second novel] and *The Bluest Eye* because they were books I had wanted to read. No one had written them yet, so I wrote them" (*Conversations* 161). Writing, however, was to come slowly. Feeling isolated while raising two sons on her own, Morrison joined a writing group and had to produce something to offer the class. Being a mother and holding a full-time job left almost no time to write; nonetheless, while she was working for Random House between 1965 and 1970, she found time to develop her short story into a publishable novel.

Among the early reviewers, Haskel Frankel, writing for the *New York Times Book Review* (November 1, 1970), called Morrison "a writer of considerable power and tenderness" and praised her well-crafted scenes of characters in painful or compromised situations and vividly rendered sense of place. He questioned, however, Morrison's choice to have Pecola, whose story is at the center of the novel, appear so frequently in the shadow of Claudia and her sister and was critical of what he called Morrison's "fuzziness born of flights of poetic imagery." What, he wondered, did she mean by "Nuns go by quiet as lust"?

Another reviewer, L.E. Sissman, writing for *The New Yorker* (January 23, 1971), said the most distinguishing feature of the novel was the fact that it was about "people to whom no ultimate glory is possible." He praised Morrison for having created a "fresh, close look at the lives of terror and decorum of those Negroes who want to get on in a white man's world— Negroes who would now be scorned as Uncle Toms [and for having put] her compassionate finger on the role of crude fantasy in sustaining hope." Sissman questioned Morrison's use of the Dick and Jane narrative and, like Frankel, deplored Morrison's "occasionally false and bombastic line."

Although *The Bluest Eye* was written during the civil rights decade, Morrison had a hard time finding a publisher, and although it was mainly well received (if not well understood), it was out of print by 1974. Perhaps readers able to take on Morrison's demanding and uncomfortable look at American society had not yet reached critical mass. According to research done by Nancy J. Peterson in *Toni Morrison: Critical and Theoretical Approaches* (1997), five years passed before a serious, scholarly treatment of the novel appeared. The first critic, Joan Bischoff, published an essay titled "The Novels of Toni Morrison: Studies in Thwarted Sensitivity" in a now-defunct publication, *Studies in Black Literature* (1975). Peterson points out that this early criticism missed the essential concerns and value of Morrison's writing and justified her stated concerns that black writers and their publications would not receive adequate recognition and scholarly attention. In a reflection included in the 1994 printing of the novel, Morrison likened the initial reception of *The Bluest Eye* to Pecola's life—"dismissed, trivialized, misread." Peterson dates the first substantive focus on Morrison's work to 1977, when a group of black intellectuals published editorial commentary in *First World*, a glossy publication devoted to developing a forum on black culture. "In their methodology and their nuanced readings of Morrison's [first novels—*The Bluest Eye* and *Sula*]," Peterson writes, these early critics

> carefully [laid] the groundwork for a criticism that locates Morrison specifically as an African-American writer—a critical approach that is so familiar to us today that it is perhaps difficult to recognize the struggle that took place to claim and articulate this methodology. (4)

Making sense of why so much time had to pass before Morrison was afforded the public acclaim her work deserves requires looking at her own seriousness about it—her novel representation of uncomfortable subject matter and insistence on her readers' participation. In the introduction to *The Cambridge Companion to Toni Morrison* (2007), critic Justine Tally asserts that in Morrison's "seminal essay," "Unspeakable Things Unspoken: The Afro-American Presence in American Literature" (1989), the author presented her challenge to readers and critics alike: "What we [who are influenced by Morrison's words] do as writers and critics is not just important; it is crucial; it is not just informative, it is formative; it is not just interesting, it profoundly shapes the perception of the world as we, and others, come to 'know' it" (*CC* 1).

This effort is precisely what Morrison intends her readers to make in *The Bluest Eye*. In her foreword to the 2007 Vintage edition, she acknowledged the possibility for misreading that might occur by "centering the weight of the novel's inquiry on so delicate and vulnerable a character [as Pecola] [that readers might be led] into the comfort of pitying her rather than into an interrogation of themselves [as complicit actors]" (xii). Earlier, she wrote, "Who told [Pecola she was ugly]? Who made her feel that it was better to be a freak than what she was? . . . The novel pecks away at the gaze that condemned her" (xi). Morrison's story is a powerful dramatic expression of the sentiment conveyed by James Baldwin in his essay, "Autobiographical Notes":

I don't think that the Negro problem in America can even be discussed coherently without bearing in mind its context; its context being the history, traditions, customs, the moral assumptions and preoccupations of the country; in short, the general social fabric. Appearances to the contrary, no one in America escapes its effects and everyone in America bears some responsibility for it. (*Notes of a Native Son*, 1955)

Critic Gurleen Grewal notes,

[S]urely the novel goes well beyond replicating stereotypes—the black man as rapist (Cholly Breedlove), the black woman as mammy (Pauline Breedlove), or the black family as fragmented. Rather, in confronting those stereotypes, it goes to the heart of the matter: to the race-based class structure of American society that generates its own pathologies. (Grewal, *Approaches to Teaching the Novels of Toni Morrison*, 118)

These critical observations point to Morrison's major literary accomplishments. Most current and recent readers and scholars appreciate the quality and depth of her social understanding as well as the degree to which her insights and writing can lead to a level of self-awareness capable of acknowledging personal complicity in the tragic consequences of racial injustice in the United States. Establishing Morrison's place in the canon of American literature has been a complex, circuitous, and often contentious process. One of her recent critics concludes:

> These days . . . it is more than inappropriate to define Morrison as "marginal," not because she has moved to the center of the canon; but because she has managed to move the center; or perhaps it would be more appropriate to say that because of her multi-faceted and untiring work, she has helped change a restricted, predominantly white, and male-centered literary world into a multicultural mosaic. (Justine Tally, Introduction to *The Cambridge Companion to Toni Morrison*, 1)

List of Characters

Claudia MacTeer is the younger of two sisters in the MacTeer family. She contributes two "voices" to the story—one as a child, one as an adult—with curiosity, compassion, and perspective, which she uses to reflect on the fate of her childhood friend, Pecola. Claudia is adventuresome, mischievous, witty, suspicious, trusting, and, above all, curious about life. The gesture she makes with her sister—to plant the marigolds for Pecola and her baby—is hopeful and compassionate and stands in contrast to the general response of the community, which views Pecola as unworthy of attention or aid.

Frieda MacTeer is the older of the sisters, less adventuresome and witty than Claudia and, in some ways, dependent on her sister for judgment, despite her reserves of general, practical information.

Pecola Breedlove is the "little-girl-gone-to-woman" in the story. She shares her family's conviction that she is ugly and unworthy but somehow has sufficient resolve to attempt a few self-help strategies, delusional and sad though they are. Of all the characters, Pecola has been most damaged by her circumstances in life, beginning with having a family incapable of normal expressions of love and protection. Nearly every event in her life leaves her a victim, and the novel examines what influences led to her fate and what influences kept her from being helped.

Mrs. MacTeer is too busy maintaining a household on meager resources to hover affectionately over her children, but her love for Claudia and Frieda is evident in the work she does to keep the family nourished, healthy, and together. One source of strength for her is her singing; pain and frustration are reworked through song to make them more manageable and understandable.

Mr. MacTeer has little verbal presence in his household, but he works hard to keep the family going and is fiercely protective of his children when it is necessary.

Rosemary Villanucci, the daughter of a white immigrant family and neighbor of the MacTeer family, is the same age as the MacTeer sisters but would rather spy on them than play. She enjoys showing off the emblems of her higher status—her family car, the Buick, and the butter on her bread—and in doing so provides one of the ways that Claudia and Frieda come to understand their place in the class structure.

Mr. Henry arrives as a boarder in the MacTeer family household. At first seemingly harmless, he eventually cannot conceal or control his sexual desires. When prostitutes are not available, he molests Frieda and is driven from the house. The sisters initially liked him because he treated them like real people and called them glamorous names.

Mr. Yacobowski, as a member of the immigrant working class, has also been marginalized by mainstream society, but as a white male, he is "allowed" to feel superior to a little black girl. His interaction with Pecola supplies the narrative with a vignette portraying the dynamics of class division in American society.

Mrs. Breedlove/Pauline, originally from the South, fails to find community, intimacy, or sustaining work in Ohio. She falls under the spell of lifestyle and beauty standards that she cannot achieve and consequently drifts into resentment, self-righteousness, and greater isolation. Cut off from any source of emotional self-nourishment, she is unable to nurture her children. Her daughter, Pecola, calls her Mrs. Breedlove and slowly succumbs to mental illness.

Mr. Breedlove/Cholly, Pauline's husband and Pecola's father, knew nothing about his father and was abandoned by his mother at four days of age. He is, nonetheless, vigorous,

23

sensual, and spirited—perhaps because he was rescued and raised by Aunt Jimmy and her warmhearted female friends—and has no trouble calling attention to himself once he leaves home after his aunt's death and enters the world. He endures two massive emotional assaults: being forced to perform sexually before an armed group of leering and jeering white men and being crudely rebuffed by his biological father, who does not want to know who he is. These wounds stay with Cholly and eventually compromise his will to live. He burns down his house and rapes his daughter and becomes the worst of the community's pariahs.

Aunt Jimmy is Cholly's aunt, who rescues him at the age of four days from the train tracks. She is a woman of great energy and warmth and, as a result, is surrounded by a bevy of older female friends who heap affection and concern onto Cholly. When she becomes ill and dies, Cholly is overwhelmed with feelings of loss but has no means of expressing them. Although Aunt Jimmy's friends would have stepped in to take charge of him, Cholly, with no immediate family members left, finds the money Aunt Jimmy has left for him and flees. She is said to have died from eating peach cobbler, but because no one else succumbed to the same affliction, the circumstances surrounding her demise will become another interesting part of her story.

Sammy Breedlove, Pecola's brother, expresses the effect of his inadequate upbringing through withdrawal, intimidation of others, and running away from home.

China, **Poland**, and **Miss Marie**—"the three merry gargoyles"—are the prostitutes who live on the floor above the Breedloves' apartment. They share a disdain for societal expectations of respectable behavior. One skinny, one fat, and one with "bandy" legs, they are "longtime" prostitutes but not of the "inadequate" kind who cannot make it on their own and "turn to drug[s] . . . and pimps to help complete their scheme of self-destruction, avoiding suicide only to punish some absent father or to sustain the misery of some silent mother" (56). Their best memories concern good meals when times allowed it and one or two particular men, but in the main they despise and abuse men. China is preoccupied with her hair, using Nu Nile, a hair straightener, to alter her appearance. Their blowzy friendliness provides Pecola with a reliable source of human interaction and enables her to ask questions about love and men, topics of growing concern to the little girl. Pecola's social reliance on the trio reveals the paucity of relationships in her life.

Geraldine is one of Morrison's "sugar-brown" southern women who come north with aspirations of merging themselves with the dominant white society and, to this end, adopt mannerisms and appearances that de-emphasize their African roots. She thinks of herself as "colored," as opposed to the "others," the slovenly, disreputable ones she disparagingly describes. When she calls the frightened and innocent Pecola "a nasty little black bitch," she is demonstrating the power of her destructive and—ultimately—self-erasing desire to be what she is not.

Louis Junior, Geraldine's son, deprived of maternal love, absorbs his self-defeating attitude from her behavior and finds himself isolated and fearful. Without essential nurturing, he develops cruel and controlling tendencies, making Pecola the target of his negative behavior.

The Fisher family provides Pauline Breedlove with employment, status, and a level of satisfaction otherwise inaccessible to her. The family is at the opposite end of the economic spectrum from the Breedloves. Being white and wealthy, they enjoy security, abundance, and the privilege of living next to a fancy (and segregated) city park. They can also afford to be "generous" to Pauline, extending praise and other small privileges. The Fishers' daughter—a blond, blue-eyed, much-fawned-over cherub—is protected and comforted in a way that Pecola, Pauline's actual daughter, never is.

Soaphead Church/Elihue Micah Whitcomb descends from a line of deluded Englishmen who think their lot will be improved by interbreeding with members of the white race. His name Soaphead refers to the particular appearance of his hair—tight and curly that held "a sheen and wave when pomaded with soap lather." Soaphead's chief attribute—besides his capacity for massive self-delusion—is his fastidiousness, which creates the necessity for a pristine and lifeless "life." In exchange for using his special powers to grant Pecola her wish for blue eyes, he asks her to "feed" (actually poison) an old dog, which she does to her and the owner's dismay. Soaphead functions mainly as an exhibit of deluded self-promotion but also and simultaneously as a member of another black family falling prey to the prevailing belief in the superiority of "whiteness." Morrison calls Soaphead a "clean, little, old man."

Velma is the high-spirited and robust young woman who stays married to Soaphead until she discovers (two months into the union) that his plans for her will be emotionally lethal.

Summary and Analysis

Henry Louis Gates Jr. calls Toni Morrison's writing "an anomaly," because it is both popular (accessible to the common reader) and difficult (worthy of and demanding close critical attention). "A subtle craftsperson and a compelling weaver of tales," he writes, "she 'tells a good story,' but the stories she tells are not calculated to please" (Preface, *Toni Morrison: Critical Perspectives Past and Present*, x). The reader encounters both these features in the initial pages of *The Bluest Eye*.

First to contend with is an extract from the now-discredited Dick and Jane reader, which millions of American schoolchildren, up until approximately the 1970s, used to learn how to read. For varying reasons, the primer fell out of favor approximately four decades ago. Prior to that, it was part of the American educational establishment, and many older adults readily recognize the characters and are able to recite specific sentences. ("See Spot run!" is the most commonly recalled example.) The reader's stories and illustrations introduced to these young, attentive minds an image of the world as a universally happy, secure, clean, and orderly place in which boys and girls behaved and the parents, who never argued or got sick, loved each other and their children every minute of every day; not only that, their pets—Spot the dog and Puff the cat—were obedient and harmlessly playful and never strayed from home.

To label these stories as unrealistic is only one of their shortcomings as literacy tools. No nonwhite individuals are portrayed; no relatives or visitors from any faraway places enter the pages. In addition, nothing was too overwhelming or confusing in Dick and Jane's world; nothing ever went wrong that was not fixable right away. However intended, these primers were perfect disseminators of cultural messages about beauty, behavior, and privilege easily assimilated by young minds intently focused on the magic of reading. The simple sentences set in motion a narrative leading to increasingly complex assumptions and expectations about the world. The readers also proved injurious to those who unrealistically and without reflection carried these images into life after school. Morrison introduces the Dick and Jane readers into her narrative to underscore this particular effect of their use as an educational tool.

The first sentences of the novel replicate a brief and conventionally written passage from the primer, followed by the same sentences minus all marks of punctuation, and finally, the same passage repeated with all spaces between the words eliminated. Morrison's alteration and distortion of the words is jarring. The repetition duplicates our own early reading experiences where sentence following sentence yielded increasing detail and understanding, but along with the memory of the drill comes the recognition of the power of words and ideas.

The primer with all its unconscious messaging and formative influences would have been used in the schools attended by Morrison's characters—Pecola Breedlove, and the MacTeer sisters, Claudia and Frieda. Throughout the novel Morrison uses other passages from the primer to highlight especially egregious contrasts and inequities found in the world she is describing, one that is in no way reminiscent of Dick and Jane's idealized realm of childhood bliss. Another possible effect of using the primer may have been to remind readers that for a significant period of time in U.S. history it was illegal to teach reading to black people.

The second indication that Morrison's "popular" story will demand and require serious consideration by the reader is the remorseful—almost apologetic—musing of a voice we come to understand is that of Claudia as an adult reflecting on the seminal event of her childhood: the fate of her friend Pecola and Claudia's own complicity in it. She is "remorseful" because Claudia and Frieda, initially Pecola's friends and protectors, later assumed a role akin to that of a midwife who had not followed all the right steps and destroyed the life she had the responsibility of protecting. Claudia laments that they could not save Pecola or her baby despite their determination to will the desired outcome into being by finding a magic formula:

saying the "right" words while planting marigold seeds in the "right" way. Later, still obsessed by the failure of their marigolds, the sisters wished they had noticed that theirs were not the only marigolds failing to bloom; even in the gardens of the white-owned homes on the Lake Erie shores the marigolds had failed to bloom that year, suggesting that in Lorain, Ohio, in 1941, something was amiss in the community. Now, as an adult, Claudia knows that the explanation for Pecola's fate—the "why" of the story—abides in a realm of human knowledge too mysterious and shocking to articulate or understand, so she resolves to do the next best possible thing, which is to tell the "how" of the story. The "why" is left for all to contemplate if, it is implied, they are brave, wise, and curious enough to divine the truth of the situation that is not readily apparent.

Claudia begins this brief introduction to her story with a phrase—"Quiet as it's kept"—that links her to the African tradition that favored story, folklore, and gossip to convey both the mystery and wisdom that informed and sustained community life. The reader immediately learns the essential facts of the story before the narrative actually begins—Pecola's rape by her father, the ensuing pregnancy and death of the baby—and concludes, under Claudia's direction, that what follows will be an account of the sisters' failure to stop the unfolding horror and how they took their inadequate understanding of it into their adult lives with all its consequences and implications.

Also important to note is that the phrase "Quiet as it's kept" was used by many black women to indicate that a secret is about to be divulged. It also assumes a measure of interest, intimacy, even conspiracy between the one sharing the gossip and the listener. Used here as the first words uttered by Claudia, the phrase functions as an invitation to the reader to participate in the ancient tradition of listening to storytellers pondering the mysteries of life. In this way, Claudia takes on a role Morrison emphasized in her own writing—that of the *griot*, who, in African folklore, is responsible for repeating and enlivening the traditional teachings in order to ensure that the essential wisdom and secrets will be transmitted through the generations.

A question that may occur to the reader is, where did Claudia, who grew up with much of the same impoverishment that was so damaging to Pecola, see her way clear to such a responsible identity? This development in Claudia is one of the major issues the novel considers. Morrison scholar Trudier Harris makes this observation:

> As storyteller, it is Claudia's job to shape the past so that it provides coherent meaning for the present audience. When she assumes that role, she identifies herself as an active tradition bearer, who, in her younger as well as her more mature manifestations, has the responsibility of putting a horrible tale into perspective. The tale is one in which the culture has been threatened from without as well as from within; it therefore takes on the form of myth. How can a people survive such assaults on them? And if they do, who will give voice to their heroic or failed efforts? (Harris, *Fiction and Folklore: The Novels of Toni Morrison*, 16)

Claudia (as a potential cipher for Morrison) knows that Pecola's story is too important not to tell and that Pecola herself has been too damaged by life to recognize that she even has a story to tell. Before she is allowed to grow up, she has "grown down" or regressed to a place where her shattered ego is fearfully and precariously living in delusions of its own making. Conditions in Claudia's childhood were similar to those in Pecola's but different enough to make possible these later reflections that seem to yield, in the act of writing itself, some measure of comprehension and personal liberation. Literacy here is a life-saving acquisition. Feelings of remorse are appropriate reactions also, but remorse, as Morrison's novel makes clear, is not enough.

Autumn

Claudia's story of growing up in Lorain, Ohio, in 1941, covers a full year, following the progression of seasons, beginning with autumn—the start of the year for school-aged children.

30

The first section is an intimate sketch of MacTeer family life with the two sisters, Claudia and Frieda, and their parents, Mr. and Mrs. MacTeer. Intimations of poverty are everywhere: the need to collect coal fragments fallen off trains onto the track, old windows that let in the cold, the need to take in a boarder, and the fact that only one room is kept lighted and warm at night. But there is also a sense of security in the home: sister bonding, maternal vigilance against childhood illnesses, a bed that finally gets warm after just the right adjustments are made, the sounds of singing, and a father, who, although taciturn and removed, provides for his family and acts instantly to protect his daughters, as he does when he learns Frieda has been molested.

Awareness of hierarchy and exclusion are central issues in the novel, experienced minimally in the domestic life but as a pervasive and insidious influence outside the home. An example in the opening of the novel is embodied in the figure of Rosemary Vilanucci, the sisters' next-door neighbor. The name "Vilanucci" identifies her as belonging to one of the white immigrant families that came to the industrial Midwest for the promise of employment. Rosemary taunts the sisters by sitting in the family Buick eating bread with butter on it. The scene is reminiscent of the dramas all children must endure in the early years of identity formation. It also functions as a portal into the divisions between people and classes and points to the destructive influence of internalizing the idealized images of the dominant culture. The black sisters are burdened with "double consciousness"—a term from the writings of W.E.B. Du Bois that refers to the two identities minority people carry with them—one of their actual self and the second as the "other" or the "object" as rendered in the eyes (or gaze) of the white person. Of this scene, critic Evelyn Schreiber writes:

> The girls—barred from Rosemary's material world (her car, her food)—respond to Rosemary's insults of exclusion with their own desire and rage. They want what Rosemary has (her bread), but they prefer to destroy her

"arrogance" and "pride of ownership." Their double consciousness emerges in their desire for the material goods while realizing the inaccessibility of them. Rather than passive acceptance of their historically designated object position, the girls physically assert their beings on Rosemary by attacking her and marring the skin that in white culture puts Rosemary above them and denies their subject status. . . . The girls internalize their place in the social world through these responses to daily encounters. (Schreiber, *Subversive Voices*, 82)

Another critic, Lisa Williams, notes that the first line— "nuns go by as quiet as lust" carries suggestions of a "sexuality that is perverse in its quiet deceptiveness that all is not what it seems." She writes:

The class differences between Rosemary Vilanucci, and Frieda and Claudia become apparent with the bread and butter she eats while they are hungry and the 1939 Buick she sits in. Their rage at her is not internalized but is aggressively acted out, and Rosemary's reaction to their anger is to offer to pull her pants down. She seems to react intuitively to their beating by feeling she should further sexualize it. The red marks on Rosemary's skin, her tears, and then her question imply that Rosemary has learned . . . that physical violence and sexuality go together. (Williams, *The Artist as Outsider*, 59, 60)

Williams points out that Rosemary, despite her mean-spirited taunting and exploitation of the class differences between her family and the MacTeers, is still just another "little girl . . . vulnerable to sexual transgression that is based on the weak preying on the weaker" (60). Morrison is cautious about judging too quickly the transgressions of others, or, rather, she insists on seeing things from multiple perspectives.

Like all children, the sisters are often mystified by the goings-on of adult life. Claudia and Frieda love to overhear their mother chattering and gossiping with her friends; they listen for secrets about members of the community and for explanations of perplexing events. When Mr. Henry shows up at their door and becomes a boarder in the household, they are unable to detect the signs of his secret appetites and general neediness because they are so pleased when he addresses them as the glamorous Hollywood stars, Greta Garbo and Ginger Rogers.

Pecola Breedlove enters the MacTeer family life as a "case"; homeless because her father, Cholly Breedlove, has burned down the family residence, she is placed by the county authorities in the MacTeers' protection until her family figures out what to do next. Pecola's arrival introduces notions of social stratification, race, and class. In Claudia's language, the Breedlove family was now "outdoors"—helpless, without means or shelter, beyond the boundary of "normal." An older Claudia remembers how, as a child, the notion of being "outdoors" was thought to be "the real terror of life"; she comments:

> There is a difference between being put out and being put out*doors*. If you are put out, you go somewhere else; if you are outdoors, there is no place to go. The distinction was subtle but final. Outdoors was the end of something, an irrevocable, physical fact, defining and complementing our metaphysical condition. Being a minority in both caste and class, we moved about anyway on the hem of life, struggling to consolidate our weaknesses and hang on, or creep singly up into the major folds of the garment. (17)

The precariousness of one's "place" in terms of class and race creates an anxious energy that permeates the novel; and the consequences of being in the "wrong" place—poor, black, bereft of one's own culture and sustaining traditions, bereft of any hope of measuring up to the expectations of the dominating culture—are so dire as to incite frantic, desperate actions. The voice of an older Claudia remembers:

> Knowing that there was such a thing as outdoors bred in us a hunger for property, for ownership. The firm possession of a yard, a porch, a grape arbor. Propertied

black people spent all their energies, all their love, on their nests. Like frenzied, desperate birds, they over decorated everything; fussed and fidgeted over their hard-won homes; canned, jellied, and preserved all summer to fill the cupboards and shelves; they painted, picked, and poked at every corner of their houses. (18)

The impoverishment in Pecola's life is starkly evident: She brings nothing with her and, when no one is looking, helps herself to three quarts of milk. The discovery of the missing milk sends Mrs. MacTeer into an indignant rant about being taken advantage of, but she stops short of accusing Pecola outright—a sign of decency and some awareness of Pecola's precarious state of mind. She knows something about being a nurturing mother.

The appearance of the Shirley Temple cup brings to the fore the vexing questions about establishing definitions of beauty and right behavior—what standards exist for definitions of beauty, how to consider racial differences in appreciating cultural beauty, and, most importantly, what consequences are associated with living under a dominant definition of beauty that minority peoples can never realize? Critic Barbara Christian writes:

In *The Bluest Eye*, the central theme is the effect of the standardized western ideas of physical beauty and romantic love not only on the black women in Lorain, Ohio, but also on the black community's perception of its worth. All of the adults in the book, in varying degrees, are affected by their acceptance of the society's inversion of the natural order. For in internalizing the West's standards of beauty, the black community automatically disqualifies itself as the possessor of its own cultural standards. (Christian, *Black Feminist Criticism*, 52)

The Shirley Temple figure—the little girl with blue eyes, golden curls, and a bright smile—was promoted in the 1930s by the "dream-making Hollywood machine" that attempted to influence people's buying and entertainment choices. In appearance and temperament, Shirley Temple was like the Jane character in the primer, a model child. Temple became an iconic child actress, appearing in many 1930s films, doing uplifting song-and-dance routines, sometimes partnering with the African-American performer Bill "Bojangles" Robinson in tap-dance routines. Attendant on her rising popularity, Shirley Temple's face began appearing—as an enticement to buy—on all sorts of consumer items. The blue-and-white cup bearing an image of her happy, dimpled face is one example.

Frieda and Pecola share an adoration of Shirley Temple that Claudia at first repudiates. She feels an "unsullied hatred" for the child star for cavorting with Bojangles who, Claudia thinks, should be *her* daddy and *her* dancing partner instead of "one of those little white girls whose socks never slid down behind their heels" (19). Claudia confesses that as a child she did not like dolls, despising the ones she got for Christmas from adults who never actually asked her what she would like to have as a gift. Claudia is soon enthralled by the idea of "dismembering" them to see if she can discover the secret of these "blue-eyed, yellow-haired, pink-skinned doll[s]," so that she might understand the mesmerizing charm they have for other people. "I did not know why I destroyed those dolls," writes Claudia. "But I did know that nobody ever asked me what I wanted for Christmas" (20). Despite the poverty of her family and the confusions and hostilities she must live with, Claudia's childhood is not bereft of joy, and she has fond memories that she has carried into adulthood.

Claudia's hatred of Shirley Temple does not last, perhaps because it separated her from the others she wanted to be close to. But "the truly horrifying thing was the transference of the same impulses to little white girls . . . and the indifference with which I could have axed them"(22). Harboring such dangerous impulses threatens her stability, and Claudia makes an accommodation—she wills herself to love Shirley Temple like everyone else, a change she wisely acknowledges was "adjustment without improvement" (23). She will need to find another way to take her stand against a set of ideals that will always undermine rather than nurture her well-being.

Pecola experiences menstruation for the first time while staying with the MacTeers. The discovery comes as a shock. Frieda—older—knows enough to persuade Pecola that she is not dying, but both sisters are scared, baffled, and thrilled at the same time and want to share Pecola's new status. Their effort to help Pecola with her new situation is performed with clumsy urgency, which gets the attention of "dough-white" Rosemary who is caught watching their antics through the fence. Seeing the "burial" of Pecola's bloody garment and the attempt to pin a napkin to her dress bring forth screams of actual or feigned alarm addressed to Mrs. MacTeer and certain to stir up trouble: "Frieda and Claudia are out here playing nasty!" Mrs. MacTeer is quick to shut down any display of "nasty," but in the course of administrating her punishment, she figures out the truth and instantly transforms herself into a nurturing mother. Her parting remark—"Go on home, Rosemary. The show is over"—shows her to be a savvy mother as well, alert, in this case, to Rosemary's mixed motives. The episode has a benign but not fully reassuring ending: The conversation among the three little girls in bed that night is inspired by the events of the day; Pecola wonders how menstruation makes babies possible. After learning from Frieda that "love" is also involved, Pecola asks, "How do you do that? I mean, how do you get someone to love you?" In and out of these scenes flows the sound of Mama's laughter and her singing—soothing and reassuring to everyone.

In the next section, we see what was formerly the Breedlove family dwelling—as sharp a contrast to the green-and-white house with the red door belonging to Dick and Jane as one could imagine. By the time of Claudia's adult observations—many years after the novel's central narrative occurs, in 1941—the house sits abandoned in an industrial section of Lorain, Ohio, that has seen more lively and prosperous days. It is a structure that neither "recedes" nor "harmonizes" with its environment but "rather foists itself on the eye of the passerby in a manner that is both irritating and melancholy" and causes visitors to town to "wonder why it has not been torn down" (33).

Readers familiar with the poems of T.S. Eliot will likely be reminded of scenes from *The Waste Land*, where the desolation and physical ugliness of modern urban sprawl predominate, and relationships between people are strained at best, sterile at worst, and always transient. Such a rendering of a northern midwestern city can be viewed as an indictment against the kind of "home" it provided the stream of black people migrating north in huge numbers from the Jim Crow South in expectation of employment and a better life. The economic realities of the times combined with the less overt northern racism undermined these expectations in many instances. Trudier Harris writes:

> The cultural beliefs that inform the storytelling in *The Bluest Eye* are manifested in a reversal of cultural health for black people, an acquiescence to destructive myths. Morrison creates an environment and a landscape in which infertility is the norm, where values with the potential to sustain have been reversed or perverted, and where few individuals have the key to transcending their inertia. Her depiction of the cycle of seasons without growth, from autumn to summer, evoke, in their mythological implications, comparisons to the legend of the Fisher King and to the world T.S. Eliot creates in *The Waste Land*. The novel is a ritualized exploration of the dissolution of culture and the need for an attendant rite of affirmation. (Harris, 27)

The description of the interior of the Breedlove home suggests and reflects the dysfunctionality of the people who had been living there. Though, as Morrison notes, the family was not so much living there as "festering together in the debris of a realtor's whim"—clearly an uncared-for place to house people regarded as unworthy of anything better. The space is so non-nurturing and incommodious that family members are not only unable to relate to one another, they cannot form pleasant associations with the physical features of the house:

[The furnishings] were anything but describable, having been conceived, manufactured, shipped, and sold in various states of thoughtlessness, greed, and indifference. The furniture had aged without ever having become familiar. People had owned it, but never known it. No one had lost a penny or a brooch under the cushions of either sofa and remembered the place and time of the loss or the finding. . . . [T]he joylessness [of the place] stank, pervading everything. (35–36)

The final part of the "Autumn" section describes the Breedlove family dynamic. Cholly Breedlove has an alcoholic stench that sickens his daughter Pecola, and his drinking renders him almost useless around the house. Mrs. Breedlove thinks of herself as a religious woman, but she is more self-righteous than religious. "[She] was not interested in Christ the Redeemer, but rather Christ the Judge," (42) and, since she thought her "Christian" duty was to punish Cholly, his unredeemable sinfulness actually served her interest in being on the righteous side of God. And "[no] less did Cholly need her. She was one of the few things abhorrent to him that he could touch and therefore hurt" (42). Fierce and physical arguments rescue the couple from complete boredom: "[The quarrels] gave substance to the minutes and hours otherwise dim and unrecalled. They relieved the tiresomeness of poverty gave grandeur to the dead rooms" (41). The conflicts impart significant damage to the next generation as well. Later in the novel, Morrison will tell these people's stories more thoroughly, leaving the reader less quick to judge. What would have happened to Cholly if his "inarticulate fury" found expression or if his "desires [had not been] aborted"? (42) What were the enduring effects of Cholly being taunted by the white men as he was engaged in an act of sexual intimacy? These kinds of considerations are distinguishing features of Morrison's writing.

Sammy Breedlove expresses himself through bursts of murderous rage aimed at his father, and Pecola, staying hidden in bed to escape the sounds of parental fighting, and suffering from nausea that might be an early sign of her pregnancy, asks God to help her become invisible. Pecola, Morrison's main focus as the person in the novel most vulnerable to societal and communal failure, wants to disappear. To this end, she has invented a mental strategy to make each part of her body disappear, except her eyes. She cannot get them to disappear, and, since they were "everything," Pecola decides that her wish to be invisible was not worth the effort.

In *The Bluest Eye*, Morrison constructs a story of two parallel lives—Pecola's and Claudia's—that develop under similar but not duplicate conditions and come (in the novel) to very different ends. Her construction of the narrative is made complex by telling the main story from Claudia's point of view simply because the adult Claudia has a perspective the confused girl Pecola does not. Claudia has two voices in the story. The primary one is her adult self looking back on the year when the marigolds failed to bloom and her friend Pecola withdrew from their common life into mental illness; the other voice is Claudia's rendering of herself as a child growing up in Lorain, Ohio. To gain access to the innermost thoughts of Pecola, Morrison also creates the voice of an omniscient narrator. This intermixing of voices with different perspectives from varying time frames is necessary for understanding as fully as possible the causes, influences, and consequences of the various actions her vivid characters take.

At the beginning of the section describing Breedlove family life, Morrison makes clear that this family has one thing in common aside from (but connected to) their shared dysfunction:

> The Breedloves did not live in a storefront because they were having temporary difficulty adjusting to cutbacks at the plant. They lived there because they were poor and black, and stayed there because they believed they were ugly. Although their poverty was traditional and stultifying, it was not unique. But their ugliness was unique. No one could have convinced them that they were not relentlessly and aggressively ugly. (39)

This is an important point Morrison conveys to her readers: Poverty by itself does not ruin people. Throughout the novel, Morrison adds to our understanding about why each member of the family has acquired a destructive and self-sabotaging attitude, but it is Pecola she chooses as her focus. She has been explicit about her reasons for concentrating on the character of Pecola. Writing in 1987, critic Stephanie A. Demetrakopoulos, discussing the way Morrison and Ralph Ellison portray the "invisibility" of the black person in the United States, points out that Morrison adds the dimension of "femaleness" to the plight of Pecola:

Pecola is . . . obstructed and deflected from higher consciousness of self because she is female. [She] is expunged from human society even before she has awakened to a consciousness of self. Pecola stands for the triple indemnity of the female Black child: children, Blacks, and females are devalued in American culture. (*New Dimensions of Spirituality*, 34)

In a passage that follows the morning scene in which Pecola hides in bed and tries to become invisible, Morrison provides the reader with access to Pecola's unspoken thoughts:

Long hours she sat looking into the mirror, trying to discover the secret of the ugliness, the ugliness that made her ignored or despised at school, by teachers and classmates alike. . . . It had occurred to Pecola some time ago that if her eyes . . . were different, that is to say, beautiful, she herself would be different. . . . If she looked different, beautiful, maybe Cholly would be different, and Mrs. Breedlove, too. Maybe they'd say, "Why, look at pretty-eyed Pecola. We mustn't do bad things in front of those pretty eyes." (46)

For an entire year, she prays to God for blue eyes. She is discouraged but not without hope: "To have something as wonderful as that happen would take a long, long time" (46).

The omniscient narrator observes: "[Convinced] that only a miracle could relieve her, she would never know her beauty. She would see only what there was to see: the eyes of other people" (47).

"The eyes of other people," this is what W.E.B. Du Bois meant by "double vision," the gaze that black people must live with and accommodate when they attempt to make a place for themselves as a minority people in a white-dominant culture. Pecola becomes the object of such a disapproving gaze when she visits the candy store with her three pennies.

Mr. Yacobowski, proprietor of his own grocery store and another member of the white immigrant population, impatiently, almost resentfully, waits on Pecola. Their "exchange" is imagined by the omniscient narrator: He decides she is unworthy of courteous service or even his glance, and she "looks up at him and sees the vacuum where curiosity ought to lodge . . . the total absence of human recognition—the glazed separateness" (48). She gets what she came for—three pieces of the candy called Mary Janes—but is denied what she more importantly needs, friendly human contact.

Mary Jane, the character for whom the candies are named, appears pictured on the wrappers, her pretty, blue-eyed face smiling mischievously. Critic Tracey L. Walters points out that within the Dick and Jane framework, the Mary Jane candies are another example of the subtle way white aesthetic values infiltrate Pecola's psyche in particular and American culture in general:

> From candy wrappers, to movie stars and dolls Pecola cannot escape the culturally promoted image of blonde hair and blue eyes. . . . Without the money to purchase skin-bleaching creams or to access colored contact lenses that allow today's Black girls to buy into the fantasy of whiteness, Pecola must find other ways to make the transition from Black to White. Pecola's resolve is to digest whiteness. She achieves this by eating Mary Jane candy . . . and drinking from a [Shirley Temple cup]. (Tracey, *African American Literature and the Classicist Tradition*, 118–119)

Pecola's next interaction, with the prostitutes China, Poland, and Miss Marie (Maginot Line), is casually friendly but insubstantial: When they ask her why she wears no socks, they do not expect or get a real answer, nor do they pursue the obvious explanation—that little necessities like socks are missing from Pecola's life either from poverty or neglect. It is with these friendly women—not, strikingly, with her own mother or other appropriate adult female—that Pecola feels sufficiently comfortable to ask questions about men, sex, and love. All she knows of love is what she has overheard: Cholly's "choking sounds" and Mrs. Breedlove's silence.

Winter

At the beginning of this section, Claudia describes her father's face using references to winter—"His eyes become a cliff of snow threatening to avalanche; his eyebrows bend like black limbs of leafless trees"—images that seem out of place in conjuring the visage of a southern man. Claudia calls him "wolf killer turned hawk fighter" and "a Vulcan guarding the flames." In an obvious contrast to Cholly, Pecola's father, Mr. MacTeer not only brings in the coal but participates in the iconic task of "keeping the home fires burning."

With memories of southern winters in their background, the characters face midwestern winters. Claudia and her family must endure their "icebox mornings" with lumpy oatmeal for breakfast, anticipating spring and the possibility of gardens. Boredom is a problem, too, but Claudia and her friends soon learn they were better off with boredom than they are with the unboring surprise they receive: the new girl in school, Maureen Peal, a "high-yellow dream girl . . . as rich as the richest of the white girls, swaddled in comfort and care." Maureen's charm sends the entire school—blacks, whites, boys, girls, and all the teachers—into a swoon of fawning. Claudia vacillates between jealousy over Maureen's clothes, especially her tight and tidy socks, and a reluctant readiness to befriend her if allowed. Maureen appears to have no flaws—a condition the sisters find unendurable, so they come up with a nickname for her, transforming Maureen Peal into Meringue Pie, and they learn that she has both an unattractive canine tooth and signs of an early disfigurement on her hands.

Morrison critics in general praise the author for her adeptness at exposing the causes and consequences of class divisions in American society. Mr. Yacobowski is one example of the subtlety of these dynamics: As an immigrant, he has himself been marginalized, but as a white male, he can marginalize ("not see") Pecola in his candy store. The appearance of Maureen Peal allows Morrison to make even more potent observations.

"The thesis of [*The Bluest Eye*]," writes Doreatha Drummond Mbalia, is that:

> racism devastates the self-image of the African female in general and the African female child in particular . . . the African's self-image is destroyed at an early age as a result of the ruling class's . . . promotion of its own standard of beauty. . . . Morrison clearly . . . understands that the concept of beauty is a learned one—Claudia . . . learns to love the . . . blue-eyed . . . doll. . . . Maureen . . . learns she is beautiful from the propaganda of the dominant society [and] from the African adult world; and Pauline . . . learns from the silver screen that every face must be assigned some category on the scale of absolute beauty. (*Toni Morrison's Developing Class Consciousness*, 32–33)

Morrison has Claudia refer to Maureen as "this disrupter of seasons"—a strong condemnation, as if she represents a force that could rearrange the design of nature itself. This disruptive presence is illustrated in the scene of Pecola's harassment by the group of black boys who use racial language to victimize her, one with whom, in a less disrupted or fractured world, they should be aligning or eager to defend. Lighter-skinned Maureen's first impulse—as the observer and not the victim, in this instance—is to sympathize with Pecola, who, with the darkest skin, is made into a target. Morrison's critical point is that the experience of living under the damaging influence of a "master" or "superior" race has, in instances, only engendered intraracial prejudice and competition resulting in crippling consequences for all. The making of such a divisive hierarchy based on economic status and skin color is harmful to everyone. Of the band of cruel boys who fling racial insults at Pecola—"Black e mo. . . . Yadaddsleepsnekked"—Morrison writes:

> They had extemporized a verse made up of two insults about matters over which the victim had no control [skin color and a parent's sleeping habits]. . . . That they themselves were black, or that their own father had similarly relaxed habits was irrelevant. It was their contempt for their own blackness that gave the first insult its teeth. They seemed to have taken all of their smoothly cultivated ignorance, their exquisitely learned self-hatred, their elaborately designed hopelessness and sucked it all up into a fiery cone of scorn that had burned for ages in the hollows of their minds—cooled—and spilled over lips of outrage, consuming whatever was in its path. (65)

Maureen's sympathy for Pecola extends into the appearance of friendship, until the possibility is snuffed out, by either bad manners or willful ignorance, when Maureen associates Pecola with a character of the same name, a mulatto girl, in the "picture show, you know" (Pecola is, of course, too poor to afford a trip to the cinema) who hates her mother for being too black and too ugly. Claudia and Frieda are also briefly drawn into this unstable quartet. Maureen leverages her power over the others (her light skin; her family's means to sue white people for acts of prejudice against them; and her apparent, albeit imperfect, understanding of babies and sex) until an "errant" comment about naked fathers quickly escalates into expressions of underlying hostility and mutual mistrust. An illuminating detail coloring this scene in the novel is the fact that Claudia had seen her father naked and had found it fascinating but not shameful. Now, after this incident, she is ashamed of being unashamed. Pecola is deeply affected as well, dealt even more humiliation and defeat, as Maureen suddenly joins the victimizers, shouting their same insults as she avoids being hit in the face by Claudia's notebook. Safely across the street, Maureen adds her own especially divisive insult: "I *am* cute! And you ugly!" (73). The three girls are left at the curbside, their "angry faces knotted like dark cauliflowers."

Parting company with Pecola, the sisters head home, heavy with a fresh, new burden: "If [Maureen] was cute—and if anything could be believed, she *was*—then we were not. And what did that mean? We were lesser. Nicer, brighter, but lesser" (74).

Looking back on this moment as an adult, Claudia sees that, having been able to draw on the relative strengths of the MacTeer family (such as they were), she and Frieda had been able to stay "in love with [themselves and] comfortable in [their own] skins" (74). They are further ennobled by this mature lifesaving insight:

All the time we knew that Maureen Peal was not the Enemy and not worthy of such intense hatred. The *Thing* to fear was the *Thing* that made *her* beautiful, and not us. (74)

Returning home, Claudia and Frieda are greeted by the troubling sight of Mr. Henry wearing only his bathrobe. He entices them with pennies for ice cream to leave the house so he can have his scheduled private tryst with the prostitutes but is discovered and confronted by the girls returning earlier than he had expected. Upon being discovered, Mr. Henry turns from the slightly overfriendly boarder into the needy and prurient older man the sisters have intuitively suspected him of being. His new personality is exposed when he tries to deflect their suspicions with his "grown-up-getting-ready-to-lie laugh" (78). The ruse fails, and the episode ends with the sisters' decisions to let the boiling turnips burn just enough to be excused from eating them and to not tell their mother about Mr. Henry because she "would just fuss all day" about it. The sisters lie so they can avoid the harsh realization of an adult exposed to be other than he initially seemed. They also enjoy Mr. Henry's friendliness even if it has a lascivious dimension, and they may not want to lose that bit of adult attention. Also emerging in this scene are rumor and gossip surrounding another adult who may also be hiding the truth. The prostitute Miss Marie, the one nicknamed "Maginot Line," is condemned for her profession, but the community takes its censure one step further, saying she has "killed people, set them on fire, poisoned them, [and] cooked them in lye" (77).

In the next section, Morrison points to the larger social context in which each of the community's black families is defining itself and setting a course for the next generation. Among the families recently arrived in Lorain, Ohio, are those who have determinedly severed all connection with their African roots and who define themselves as "coloreds." Morrison describes the women who dominate these families:

> These sugar-brown Mobile girls . . . wash themselves with orange-colored Lifebuoy soap, dust themselves with Cashmere Bouquet talc . . . straighten their hair with Dixie Peach, and part it on the side. . . . They go to land-grant colleges, normal schools, and learn how to do the white man's work with refinement: home economics to prepare his food; teacher education to instruct black children in obedience; music to sooth the weary master and entertain his blunted soul. Here they learn . . . how to behave. (83)

Morrison warns that what is lost in this "self-cleansing" process of appropriating white lifestyles and attitudes is nothing less than the essential selves of these people, their wholeness, their distinctive "funkiness." Any sign or eruption of the "funkiness of passion . . . nature [and] the wide range of human emotions" must be expunged: "the laugh that is a little too loud"; "the enunciation a little too round"; "the gesture a little too generous." They are instead preoccupied with making a clean, orderly, and respectable home. They marry men who appreciate their efforts, and they have children; they tolerate but do not enjoy sex. Joy, in fact, seems fairly absent in all aspects of their lives.

46

Geraldine is one such woman. She lives with her family: her husband, Louis; her son, Junior; and her cat, who, because Geraldine has apparently alienated herself from the realm of human interaction, "will always know that he is first in her affections" (86). The cat gets the only physical attention Geraldine is prepared to give or receive—a relocation of intimacy that deprives her son, Junior, and drives him to acts of cruelty and other behaviors certain to bring about a disturbed and friendless childhood. Junior had earlier longed to be a normal kid, a normal "black" kid, but he learned from his mother to cautiously select his companions and ended up "alternately bored and frightened at home."

The "Winter" section of the novel ends with a distressing scene that illustrates the destructive and self-destructive consequences of living under these artificial and repressed conditions. With nothing better to do, Junior entices Pecola into his house with the promise of seeing "his kittens" and the possibility of taking one home. Pecola knows enough to be hesitant but is quickly drawn into the house by its "beautiful" appearance. Geraldine's house reflects a particular style. Unrestrained in her effort to appear respectable, as others have defined it, she has chosen to adorn the house with a wealth of doilies, houseplants, and framed pictures decorated with fake flowers. Standing, mesmerized by this display, Pecola is startled when Junior suddenly throws the cat at her face, leaving her scratched and frightened. When she tries to flee, Junior displays the kind of frenzied and controlling behavior, which, combined with the presumably fatal blow he next inflicts on the cat, is indicative of antisocial pathology. When Geraldine arrives on the scene to find her inert cat on the floor, she looks at Pecola—dirty torn dress, unruly hair, muddy shoes—and instantly assumes the little girl from an impoverished family is the culprit: "She had seen this little girl all of her life. . . . They were everywhere. They slept six in a bed, all their pee mixing together in the night as they wet their beds. . . . [They] idled away, picking plaster from the walls. . . . [They] crowded into pews at church, taking space from the nice, neat, colored children" (92).

This scene illustrates the virulent influence of the divisive stereotyping of others and of blind subservience to appearances. Mbalia writes:

> When Geraldine sees Pecola, she is reminded of everything she has sought to escape—everything associated with the poor, struggling African masses. . . . [Calling] Pecola, a little girl of ten, a "nasty little black bitch" and commanding her to "get out of my house" illustrate the extent of Geraldine's isolation from her people and her association with her oppressors. (Mbalia, 35)

Another critic, Jan Furman, makes a further point:

> To Pecola, Geraldine is the "pretty milk-brown lady in the pretty gold and green house" [and to] Morrison, she is a shadow image of the Dick-and-Jane life, a sadistic approximation of the storybook people. Through her Morrison demonstrates that such a life as Geraldine's is only validated by the exclusion of others. (Furman, *Toni Morrison's Fiction*, 15)

Spring

Morrison opens this section of the novel with an image of new life with its extraordinary resilience for adaptation: "the first twigs are thin, green, and supple. They bend into a complete circle, but will not break" (97). These new twigs, as it turns out, exist in Claudia's memory as mechanisms of punishment, but they also suggest the resilience of early plant growth as similar to that of a young human life ready to withstand the inevitable challenges of growing up. With the wrong conditions or too little nurturing, however, neither twig nor child grows properly. One example of these "wrong conditions" is the inappropriate expression of sexual desire. Claudia begins her spring recollections with an instance of sexual violation.

Returning from some private time in the long springtime grass, where she has been enjoying imaginative reveries about matters of life and death, Claudia finds things amiss at home. Mr. Henry, deprived of his association with the prostitutes, has molested Frieda by touching her breasts. Claudia's love of drama gets the better of her as she eagerly asks for all the details of what Mr. Henry actually did and how Frieda felt about it. Frieda is in shock, and Claudia finally has the sense to admit, "I wasn't asking the right questions," but nothing can dull her enthusiasm for the darkly comic aftermath. Papa MacTeer throws a tricycle at Mr. Henry, which knocks him off the porch and somehow induces him, after getting back on his feet, to sing the hymn, "Nearer My God to Thee," shortly before getting hit in the head again, this time by a broom wielded by Mrs. MacTeer. A neighbor rushes in with a gun, in response to the clamor, and Mr. MacTeer takes the weapon, not heeding his wife's screams, and shoots at Mr. Henry, who jumps in fright out of his shoes and flees in his socks, all to the sounds of everybody "cussing and screaming." "Oh, shoot, I always miss stuff," laments Claudia. This blending of the horrors of child sexual abuse with an almost slapstick routine of physical comedy gestures to the complexity and completeness of Morrison's realist vision. It also underscores all the more that some individuals, such as Pecola, have no advocates with a stake at protecting their innocence and well-being.

From her mother's talk, Frieda now believes she's a "ruined" woman like the prostitutes, and this new fear sends the sisters in search of Pecola. In their inimitable children's logic, they think being "ruined" means being fat, a condition that is "cured" by drinking whisky, which Pecola has because "her father's always drunk." Eventually they trace Pecola to the fancy home where her mother, Pauline, works but not before an encounter with Maginot Line, who punishes their "attitude" by hurling a glass soda bottle at them. The sisters head off to find Pecola, despite their certainty that straying too far from their part of town will not please their mother. In what amounts to a definition of "security" for the MacTeer sisters, they dismiss the fear of "mama gone get us" with the assurance that only a whipping awaits them: "That was true," Claudia says, "she couldn't kill us, or laugh a terrible laugh at us, or throw a bottle at us" (105).

The scene outside Pauline's place of employment speaks of exclusivity, ease, and wealth; landscaped yards, newly painted houses, and clusters of trees form the neighborhood, and the house they are seeking turns out to be located near the entrance to Lake Shore Park, a well-manicured public space reserved for white, not black, families. Inside the house, shiny white porcelain, painted woodwork, polished cabinets, and "brilliant copperware" all bask in the aroma of ample, properly prepared food. This is the household of the Fishers, Pauline's employer, and another example of family life in Lorain, Ohio. All three girls stand as if starstruck at the sight of the picture-book kitchen, but the scene quickly devolves into chaos when Pecola accidentally knocks the freshly baked fruit cobbler to the floor. In an egregious display of maternal failure and child abuse, Pauline reacts to her spoiled dessert by angrily knocking her daughter down and indignantly throwing the three "miscreants" out of the "perfect house." Pauline's maternal instincts to comfort and reassure a small child are directed at the Fishers' yellow-haired, beribboned daughter who has burst into tears over this disruption to her afternoon. Pauline's self-worth is so completely defined by her role as the "ideal servant" to this prosperous white family that she chooses to preserve that false identity rather than come to the rescue of her own daughter.

Once again, Morrison depicts unnatural and shocking behavior by a character she then labors to explain. The voice of the omniscient narrator intermingled with Pauline's stream-of-consciousness monologue exposes the unsure footing her life began on—literally a malformed foot caused by stepping on a rusty nail, an injury neglected, we can assume, by her poor or uninformed parents. Many things about Pauline's life do not go the way she wants, and she uses her imperfect foot as an explanation. The ninth of eleven children, Pauline must have grown up with a chaotic and inadequate family life, so that later, possibly in compensation, she becomes especially devoted to keeping things in proper order. Her formative years were also characterized by hard work and emotional isolation, factors that potentially explain why she is so receptive to the hymns she hears in church, the ones in which a being of total love and understanding for each soul offers solace and companionship. Her favorite begins: "Precious Lord take my hand / Lead me on, let me stand. . . . Hear my cry hear my call / Hold my hand lest I fall."

Pauline's recollection of coming under the spell of Cholly for the first time is lush and reverential, as if she was meeting the savior who animates her spiritual life. Throughout her life, the colors of nature have been important to Pauline. She has an artistic sense but no means of expressing it or strengthening her life by connecting with and expressing her authentic roots. Cholly brings color, energy, and intimacy to her life, putting Pauline temporarily in the throes of romance. She recalls:

When I first seed Cholly . . . it was like all the bits of color from that time down home when all us chil'ren went berry picking . . . and I put some in the pocket of my Sunday dress, and they mashed up and stained my hips. My whole dress was messed with purple, and it never did wash out. Not the dress nor me. I could feel that purple deep inside me. (115)

Pauline and Cholly fall in love; he was "kind and lively," caused more laughter than she knew was in the world, and he treated her deformed foot as an "asset." With her family, Pauline had already moved north to Kentucky, where she and Cholly met. From there, after agreeing to marry, they decide to continue the migration and head farther north to Ohio to find work and establish a home. This hopeful and excited Pauline is the same woman who, a few pages earlier, sent her daughter away after knocking her down. What occasioned such a radical transformation in this once kind, hopeful woman?

Of this general migration, Barbara Christian writes:

Migration from the rural South to a more or less urban North has had great impact on the lives of Afro-Americans . . . [the effect of which] on the characters . . . is a major consideration in *The Bluest Eye*. Morrison [introduces]

Lorain, Ohio as a land that would allow neither the marigolds nor Pecola to grow. . . . [The novel's characters] are recent arrivals . . . whose connection to another place, the South, had been intense and life-sustaining if only because they'd had to forge a tradition of survival against great odds. As new inhabitants, and as black people, they are looked down upon by the more established white community. . . . The black migrants must therefore learn to survive in this land that is at present a sterile one for them, even as they try to evolve a tradition that is functional in this place. Until they do, their lives will lack coherence. (Christian, *Black Feminist Criticism*, 48)

Christian goes on to show how Pauline's life is representative of this loss. As one cut off from her own sustaining roots, she becomes easy prey to the Hollywood-driven and commercial promotions of standards of desirable beauty and respectable lifestyles. The trouble she has making friends with women who are disdainful of her unstraightened hair and her way of talking and dressing, combined with her declining intimacy with Cholly, drive Pauline to dress stores and the "silver screen." "The sad thing was that Pauline did not really care for clothes and makeup. She merely wanted other women to cast favorable glances her way" (118).

Pregnancy temporarily eases relations between Pauline and Cholly, but the loneliness persists—an isolation she recognizes as different from the loneliness experienced back home. She fails to recognize that her loneliness in the North is an "emptiness," partly rooted in cultural displacement and partly caused by her inability to value her own heritage. For solace, she goes to the movies where

in the dark her memory was refreshed, and she succumbed to her earlier dreams. Along with the idea of romantic love, she was introduced to another—physical beauty. Probably the most destructive ideas in the history of human thought. Both originated in envy, thrived in insecurity, and ended in disillusionment. . . . She was never able, after her education in the movies, to look at a face and not assign it some category in the scale of absolute beauty. (122)

Falling under the influence of such judgment and divisiveness leaves Pauline un-nurtured and self-punishing. The rest of her monologue confirms this change. After accidentally losing a tooth, she lets go of her incipient hope of making herself beautiful and settles "down into just being ugly." Becoming a first-time parent is tiring, but she wants another child and vows to love it no matter its appearance. In imaginative and endearing language, Pauline talks to not-yet-born Pecola, forming a bond with her second child and a promise to make things different. But newborn Pecola turns out to have "pretty hair, but Lord she was ugly."

The narrator returns to explain how Pauline attempted to rescue herself by realigning with the church but not, as before, through the stirring hymns and a comforting sense of Jesus as a loving companion. Instead, she embraces a self-righteous pre-occupation with other people's sins and the harsh punishments that await them: "Holding Cholly as a model of sin and failure, she bore him like a crown of thorns, and her children like a cross" (127). With such dissatisfaction at home, Pauline satisfies her need for purpose, orderliness, and belonging by throwing herself into her work as the Fisher family's ideal servant in their ideal family home, which effectively eclipses and replaces her own storefront home: "More and more, she neglected her house, her children, her man [who became] like afterthoughts one has just before sleep" (127).

Pauline's story is marked by a sense of waste and inner turbulence. She was once a person with a dreaming and artistic sensibility. She was also a hard worker. She has become a mother with nothing to give her children except advice to not be like their father, and she offers no reason for her children to bond with her. Unconsciously she causes Pecola to internalize the attitudes and perceptions that devalue her and lead her to "grow down" instead of up. By giving Pauline her own voice, Morrison allows her careworn mother figure to speak of the tragedy she perceives her life to be. According to Barbara Christian, Morrison has created "the first evocation of a black domestic's inner voice" (Christian, from *Toni Morrison: Critical and Theoretical Approaches*, 30).

Having learned about Cholly Breedlove through Pauline's eyes, the reader is then furnished with the narrator's more objective insights. Cholly, we already know, has burned down his house and raped his daughter. This should be enough for instant and irrevocable condemnation, and there is nothing Morrison does in portraying Cholly's actions that make them less despicable; remarkably, in her hands, his story evokes substantial empathy as well as repulsion.

Of all the characters, Cholly has the most unlikely and inauspicious of beginnings. His Aunt Jimmy, an elderly but still robust and large-hearted woman, rescued Cholly from the train tracks when he was four days old, abandoned by both parents. Jimmy becomes the center of her circle of like-minded female friends, and it is this communal upbringing that saves Cholly from complete bitterness and despair. Cholly grows up to become vigorous, sensual, respectful, and, although shy, able to draw attention to himself both for his robust appearance and his willingness to work.

After the funeral for Aunt Jimmy—expressing the "grief over the waste of life, the stunned wonder at the ways of God, and the restoration of order in nature at the graveyard"— Cholly gets caught up in the carnival-like, postfuneral spirit. After eating too much and suffering a small episode of public humiliation, he disappears into the countryside with Jake, possibly a cousin of his, and two young women. A few moments after Cholly and Darlene express their newfound intimacy, they are discovered by a band of racist white raccoon hunters with guns and flashlights who order Cholly to "perform" before their eyes to the sound of their jeering and crude insults.

This much larger humiliation Cholly endures with great difficulty:

> Sullen, irritable, he cultivated his hatred of Darlene.
> Never once did he consider directing his hatred toward

the hunters. Such an emotion would have destroyed him. They were big, white, armed men. He was small, black, helpless. His subconscious knew what his conscious mind did not guess—that hating them would have consumed him. (151)

Cholly, fourteen years old, and already six feet tall, runs away to Macon, the nearest "big city" in Georgia, intending to locate his father. He meets up with a surly gambler bearing the name Aunt Jimmy had recollected years earlier, but the encounter is devastating, ending in rejection and another humiliation too huge for him to absorb. So the young man runs until he has outdistanced everything familiar to him. Morrison concludes:

The pieces of Cholly's life could become coherent only in the head of a musician. . . . Only a musician would sense, know, without even knowing that he knew, that Cholly was free. Dangerously free. Free to feel whatever he felt—fear, guilt, shame, love, grief, pity. Free to be tender or violent. (159)

Tenderness and violence characterize the terrible mix of feelings that Cholly experiences just before he rapes his daughter. Arriving home in a drunken stupor, he comes upon Pecola washing the dishes, frail in body, raggedly dressed, and thinks: "Why did she have to look so whipped? She was a child—unburdened—why wasn't she happy?" (161) A rush of feeling washes over Cholly as he realizes how much his daughter needs and deserves and how impotent he is to provide anything of use to her. Lynn Orilla Scott writes:

The . . . incest scene occurs at the end of the chapter describing the father's life and is rendered entirely from the father's point of view. The reader views the father's act not as an assertion of power, but as the culmination of his tortured experiences with love and intimacy—experiences that in many ways parallel his daughter's. (Scott, *James Baldwin and Toni Morrison*, 88)

The scene of Pecola's rape is stark and graphic. She is shocked, baffled, helpless, and violated. She cannot utter a word, only a sound, "a hollow suck of air in the back of her throat . . . like the rapid loss of air from a circus balloon"; she falls down and feels a severe and unfamiliar pain before fainting.

None of the details Morrison provides that provoke empathy for Cholly's life can effectively mitigate the injustice of the horror he has visited on his daughter. The scene has provoked diverse and competing critical responses and perspectives. Early feminist readers were not comfortable with Morrison's approach, but the author's motives for writing had always been explicitly to ask of such acts of violation and transgression: Where does the fault really lie? Her aim was to "bear witness"; she wanted to explain, not to blame. "In Morrison's writing," observes Jan Furman, "there are no easy villains to hate; there are no predictable behaviors" (Furman, 18).

Soaphead Church is Morrison's last main player to influence the fate of Pecola. A "cinnamon-eyed West Indian," Soaphead has the educational ability to learn the meaning of the word *misanthrope* but not the experiences or opportunity to avoid being one himself. As with other self-deluded Morrison characters with disturbed personalities, Soaphead has learned to see his antipathy for other people as a virtue; it was, he determines, a means of developing character: "when he subdued his revulsion and occasionally touched, helped, counseled, or befriended somebody, he was able to think of his behavior as generous and his intentions noble" (164). Soaphead failed in his plan to become a priest and thus fools himself into thinking he prefers pursuing a profession with a seemingly important title but that actually requires neither talent nor hard work: He becomes a "Reader, Advisor, and Interpreter of Dreams." Morrison's gift for satire is on full display here. Soaphead has neatly provided himself with the "opportunity to witness human stupidity without sharing it or being compromised by it, and to nurture his fastidiousness by viewing physical decay" (165). This fastidiousness leaves Soaphead at a loss: Whom will he consort with? His choice has narrowed down to little girls—the least "tainted."

Soaphead's family background gives Morrison another chance to illustrate the effects of colonialism on black people, causing them to lose their way by denying their African roots in exchange for a "preferred status." Soaphead descends from Sir Whitcomb, a black Englishman who fathered a line of biracial progeny who proceeded—zealously—to produce additional offspring with whites to "cleanse" themselves of any sign of their former blackness. Soaphead, originally named Elihue Micah Whitcomb, descended from this lineage, going on to acquire new levels of misunderstood and misapplied education. He remembers, for example, "Hamlet's abuse of Ophelia, but not Christ's love of Mary Magdalene; Hamlet's frivolous politics, but not Christ's serious anarchy" (169). He married Velma, "a lovely, laughing, big-legged girl . . . with [so much] affection and zest for life [that] two months into the marriage [she learned of his interest] in altering her joy to a more academic gloom [and fled] the soundless cave of Elihue's mind" (170).

Soaphead comes to the United States—Lorain, Ohio, specifically—after failing at seminary and then at psychiatry because "the subject required too much truth, too many confrontations, and offered too little support to a failing ego" (170). He passes himself off as a "minister" and practices a counseling service specializing in dread: "People came to him in dread, whispered in dread, wept and pleaded in dread [and] dread was what he counseled" (172). They come with diverse and bizarre requests, such as "Make my mother give me back my clothes. . . . Keep my baby's ghost off the stove." Curiously, Soaphead responds to each request without regard for its worthiness, necessity, or even its legality.

Pregnant and banned from attending school, Pecola, her mental stability in question, comes to Soaphead in search of a miracle. With his well-advertised supernatural powers, perhaps he can give her the blue eyes that will "fix" her life, her last chance, she has convinced herself, for an imagined happiness. Soaphead hears her request and feels a benign impulse to help her and an appropriate frustration with himself for having only the pretense of power. His goodwill is short lived; it ends when he thinks of a way to trick Pecola into helping him get rid of his landlady's dog while she believes she is actually enacting a miracle. The dog, "old Bob," unkempt in ways particularly offensive to Soaphead, is an essentially harmless creature cared for by an old woman with no other companions. Poisoning the dog is an act that is cruel to the animal and the landlady but also to the trusting Pecola, who unwittingly offers poisoned meat to the dog and pats its head, until, in horror, she watches it convulse and die. Morrison has given us both a cat and a dog story in her novel that are a grotesque reworking of the stories of Puff and Spot, the faithful, perfect pets from the Dick and Jane readers.

The "Spring" section of the novel ends with Soaphead, pleased to be rid of the dog and feeling no qualms about how it was accomplished, addressing a letter to God, "HE WHO GREATLY ENOBLED HUMAN NATURE BY CREATING IT." The letter is initiated by Soaphead's satisfaction with himself for having outdone God by granting Pecola her wish for blue eyes, as he had promised, when she agreed to feed the dog. As his pride swells, however, the letter turns into a vehicle for Soaphead to chastise God for overlooking things he should be noticing and for making an imperfect world to begin with. Soaphead tries to impress God with his wide familiarity with world geography and moves on to indignantly complain that Velma had left him "the way people leave a hotel room." A hotel room being essentially a temporary, impersonal, and inconsequential place, a place one passes through to get to important destinations, the comparison serves as an egregious insult he has endured all these years. Two confessions follow— one general, one specific (his irrepressible attraction to little girls' breasts, an attraction he seems to blame on God). He appears to be simultaneously reporting on and confessing to his "parties" with little girls that may have resulted in some legal troubles for him in the past. Soaphead's letter devolves into incoherence, as he confuses God with Popeye at one point. He ends by accusing God of going off the track: "You forgot Lord ['forgot' the sad little girls—'charred, lame, halt,' crying next to their dead mothers]. You forgot how and when to be God" (181). Exhausted with his saintly efforts to help Pecola and inform God about the deed, Soaphead becomes sleepy and goes to bed. Ever deluded, he has managed to convince himself that he has ascended to a place of power and saintliness greater than that occupied by God.

Summer

In a conversation with Robert Stepto, recorded in *Toni Morrison: Playing with Difference*, Morrison makes one of her many comments in praise of women:

> Black women have held, have been given . . . the cross. They don't walk near it. They're often on it. And they've borne that, I think, extremely well" (46).

A much longer tribute appears in *The Bluest Eye* following the scene of M'Dear's visit to Aunt Jimmy's bedside to administer her "wise woman" healing powers. Morrison notes the circle of strong women who come to the rescue of Aunt Jimmy, in this instance, and all "Aunt Jimmys" everywhere—anyone in pain or distress or burdened with work. She then fills two pages describing female fortitude and selflessness. The old women "[blended] their voices into a threnody of nostalgia about pain":

> They hugged the memories of illnesses to their bosoms . . . in fond remembrance of pains they had endured— childbirth, rheumatism, croup, backaches, piles. All of the bruises they had collected from moving about the earth—harvesting, cleaning, hoisting, pitching, stooping, kneeling, picking—always with young ones underfoot. . . . Then they [became] old. . . . They had carried a world on their heads. They had given over the lives of their own children and tendered their grandchildren. [Now] they were through with lust and lactation, beyond tears and terror. . . . They were, in fact and at last, free. And the lives of these old black women were synthesized in their

eyes—a puree of tragedy and humor, wickedness and serenity, truth and fantasy. (138–139)

When Claudia begins the final section of her story, she is older, though not yet an old woman, and has arrived at a place of her own wisdom and perspective. Morrison has presented us with the stories of two parallel lives. The last words the reader hears from Pecola are delusional—a conversation she is having with an imaginary friend because her family and community have failed to provide her with the self-esteem necessary to make and sustain a genuine relationship with anyone. What brought about these very different outcomes?

One hint comes in the memory of a vision Claudia has of her own mother as she prepares to tell the last part of the story. Claudia's mother is left standing in the wake of a tornado that sweeps through their town: "She is strong, smiling, and relaxed while the world falls down about her" (188–189). These images of strong and enduring women, of mothers who labor unceasingly to promote and ensure the well-being of others, form the foundation for *The Bluest Eye*. Throughout the novel, the reader is presented with mothers in different situations— those in Claudia's neighborhood struggling with economic insecurity, each seeking a way to establish her own and her family's identities, each looking for physical and cultural nourishment. Despite their poverty, the MacTeer family has achieved a form of stability with both mother and father contributing to and protecting the family life. In Claudia's memory of childhood, there are whippings and censure to endure, chores and responsibilities, restrictions and warnings, the wrong Christmas presents, too many meals featuring turnip greens, identity and class confusion, the pressure to accept subservience in the social hierarchy of Lorain, and many scary and perplexing events. But always in the background are the sounds of her mother's singing and the accompanying assurances of "love, thick and dark as Alaga syrup" (12).

In the novel, sounds of singing interweave with—and express and deflect—some of the pain of life. Lisa Williams writes:

As [Claudia] hears her mother sing of those bad times she's endured, [she] realizes that "misery colored by the greens and blues in my mother's voice took all of the grief out of the words and left me with a conviction that pain was not only endurable, it was sweet." . . . Through her song, Claudia's mother communicates to her daughter the beauty of the African-American folk tradition of storytelling. By listening and then speaking, Claudia becomes a modern-day griot who affirms, as she participates in storytelling, the culture that the white society would like to destroy. Her positive self-identity is nurtured by her continuing relation to a maternal oral tradition (Williams, 62).

Some things, Morrison has reminded us, can be made sense of only through the eyes of an artist. Through her singing wisdom and sometimes overly harsh protectiveness, Mrs. MacTeer has enabled her daughter to choose self-preservation over self-destruction.

As Claudia tells of how she and Frieda go door to door selling seeds to get money for a new bicycle, we see how the protective rules their mother has put in place restricting how far they can go can be reasonably (although deceptively) dismissed, as the girls feel sufficiently safe and secure to stray into unfamiliar territory. They encounter no dangers and are, in fact, invited into some of the homes for cold lemonade and a rest.

While they are experiencing these manifestations of community support, they overhear the gossip about Pecola, which is related entirely in tones of condemnation that convey the absence of community support for the child. Claudia recalls:

They were disgusted, amused, shocked, outraged, or even excited by [Pecola's] story. But we listened for the one who would say, "Poor little girl" . . . but there was only head-wagging where those words should have been. (190)

The sisters learn through this same chain of gossip that Pauline gave Pecola a beating when she was told of the rape and Cholly has since disappeared. No one claims to know "these people"; they are truly "outside," banished from the circle of compassion and communal support. The Breedloves suffer from double rejections—from themselves, believing themselves to be ugly and therefore unworthy, and from the community.

The bits of community conversation that Claudia assembles for the reader vividly convey the narrowness of understanding displayed by the townspeople. Of Cholly, one asks, "What you reckon make him do a thing like that?" "Beats me," says another, "Just nasty." These are the simplistic conclusions people come up with to distance themselves from the reality of other people's lives. Morrison shows her readers that these mechanisms of self-protection are not only self-righteous, they are reminders of the countless ways people do not see or bear witness properly (as Mr. Yacobowski had failed to "see" Pecola). The people who make up Pecola's community do not use their vision, insight, or compassion to imagine lives different from their own. Morrison's vision, however, is not ultimately bleak or irredeemable. She is not a judgmental author. She shows how Claudia and Frieda have been able to internalize an ethical and humanitarian imperative, while others have not. Locating blame is not part of her authorial task. As Barbara Christian writes:

> How Pecola comes to want blue eyes demands more than just telling Pecola's story. . . . Pecola's desire is more than the result of her personal story. It encompasses three hundred years of unsuccessful interface between black and white culture. Morrison's dilemma . . . is that she cannot retell three hundred years; she must make Pecola's story relevant to that history . . . and create both a sense of intimacy . . . yet enough distance to give the theme its expansive substance. (Christian, 60)

In response to the failure of the community, the sisters decide to take on its task of supporting all of its members. "So it is with confidence, strengthened by pity and pride, that we decided to change the course of events and alter a human life" (191).

Familiar with the power of ritual, they devise their own and implement it with the best sacrifice they can make: With the seeds they plant to help Pecola's baby live, they bury their bicycle money to show that "[they] really mean it this time." (192)

Pecola's reality, however, is too far compromised for a child's ritual to repair or restore. Deserted by all, she has in her mental illness and deep despair "invented" a friend. Together they walk the back streets and vacant lots together discussing Pecola's new blue eyes.

Claudia's words conclude the novel, indicative of the hard-won knowledge—both in general and of the self—she has arrived at. "So it was. A little black girl yearns for the blue eyes of a little white girl, and the horror at the heart of her yearning is exceeded only by the evil of its fulfillment" (204). When the marigolds failed to bloom and Pecola's sanity erodes after the death of her baby, Claudia thought it was her fault for planting the seeds too deeply. She took responsibility for the failure, but it was neither rational nor accurate for her to be the lone guilty party. She knows that the terrible guilt is shared—by everyone, including by those most damaged. She chastises herself for her part in the failure and makes clear that she will never be at peace about what she has witnessed. Morrison said about her novel that she wanted her readers—white and black—to feel the tragedy and waste of Pecola's life, not for the purpose of congratulating themselves for having compassion but rather for accepting part of the responsibility for it.

Critical Views

STEPHANIE A. DEMETRAKOPOULOS ON MORRISON'S BLEAK VISION AND ITS REDEMPTION

Morrison places the novel in 1941 at the end of the Great Depression when life was hard for everyone, but even worse for Black people. . . .

The darkest and most permeating archetype of the novel is what I would name "Demeter Denied." And Morrison presses this on us unsparingly. An ancient Greek goddess, Demeter is in charge of the earth's fertility and its seasons; she is a major face of the Earth Mother, and her bond to her daughter Persephone symbolizes loving, cosmic on-goingness, a feminine ground of being.[4] But the novel rejects the cyclicality of time as a healing force and rejects nature as a primal force that can nurture and rejuvenate. The chief narrator of the novel, Claudia, and her older sister Frieda plant marigold seeds the year that Pecola's father Cholly rapes and impregnates Pecola; shortly thereafter she miscarries and goes mad. Pecola is both the major protagonist and Morrison's symbol of utter human desolation. In the prologue, Claudia says that the earth, like Pecola, refused to grow the planted seeds; she closes the novel with the image of Pecola wandering, lost in madness at the edge of their town among refuse and sunflowers. Marigolds and sunflowers are gold, symbolic in alchemy of psychic and sacred wholeness. They are also flowers that image how the vegetative force of the earth quickens and rises towards the sun, following it with "trust," literally turning towards it. But the ungrown, sterile marigold seeds symbolize Morrison's sense of the earth as untrustworthy, contingent, penurious, grudging. In this novel there is no cosmic ground of being that mothers us all; time is fluent and so much human and natural potential is irrevocably lost. The final vision of Pecola mad and lost amidst the garbage, yet juxtaposed to the sunflowers, is a metaphysically surreal jolt. Nature's lower life-forms (flowers) reemerge cyclically, but nature has no hierarchical values to her sustenance; she is amoral and cares not at all if higher developed creatures go mad or become altogether extinct.

Not only does Morrison reject the possibility of the earth's motherliness as a viable ground of being, she rejects the natural impulses of human beings themselves as forces to have faith in. By rejecting the seasons, the earth, human society, she exposes the romanticism of faith in these abstractions. The human body itself, and mother–daughter bonding, also are revealed as killers not healers. Since the mother–daughter dyad, as imaged in Demeter and Persephone/Kore, is so central to feminine identity, spirituality and affirmation, this resounding rejection is all the more powerful in a novel authored by a woman. Morrison's images of the human body are radically scatological. The novel opens with a story of Claudia vomiting in her bed. The childhood of Cholly, Pecola's father, features Aunt Jimmy's chamberpot reeking fumes out from under her bed into the whole house. Masculine libido deflects into child-molesting and incest. The seasons themselves are experienced by the children as different styles of whipping, and Pecola's family life (the ground of being, the mother-body of a child's existence) is defined by what degree of violence her parents daily mount against each other. Thus unpleasant truths about being embodied are forced on us repeatedly—truths we erase with technology and sanitation. What animal life we see is also far from agents of the "Peaceable kingdom;" a malevolent local minister, Soaphead Church, manipulates Pecola into killing a sickly, diseased old dog who represents to him the horror of incarnation itself; a little boy from a structured, stifling home kills his mother's cat and blames Pecola.

Imagery of hope does exist within the family, but only in the most minimal form because the adults themselves are so overwhelmed with the struggle for survival. Claudia's mother, Mrs. MacTeer, scolds her children when they get sick, threatening to sap her energy so constantly depleted by the struggle for survival. But she does care for them, and part of Claudia's life urge is in the tactile memory of her mother's hand on her feverish forehead in the middle of the night—a loving mother's touch that belies the antagonistic, angry mother of the daytime. Claudia's father is silent, taciturn, but he is also the protective Vulcan, the keeper of the fires that warm his family. He is a fond father in his quiet way, smiling when the family boarder admires his daughters. But most important is his protectiveness, which shows how significant his girls' lives are to him. When the boarder sexually molests Frieda, Claudia's father goes into a rage and has to be stopped from killing him. So there is a backdrop of strong and caring but stressed adults in the sisters' childhood. There are also some adult examples of *joie de vivre* as embodied in the gossip of the mother and her friends and their laughter as they recount the foibles of their neighbors. Also, the mother does take in Pecola for a while, though she is understandably grudging about the expense. Nevertheless, Claudia's memories are mostly dark, and her sense of life as an adult telling the tale of Pecola is bitter, fraught with anguish. Claudia is a survivor in the same sense as the witness who tells Job what he has lost; she survives only to tell us what has been lost. . . .

Morrison shows us the love of order, the aesthetic response to it in Pauline, Pecola's mother; Cholly too had artistic potential as a musician. These seeds rot and fester in the lives of the parents; Pecola's brother leaves to rove the country as lost as his father before him. Everyone surrounding Pecola is finally as lost as she. The ungrown marigold seeds of the prologue reemerge in the final imagery of the sunflowers around the mad Pecola—this form insists that this female victim, with her poetic, inward nature, is lost, expunged forever, her voice and story lost. In this first novel, there is no room for epiphany, no possibility of reaching even for inner wholeness such as Nel has at the end of *Sula*. There is only recognition of loss, irrevocable loss.

Yet for me as a reader—though surely not for Morrison as she wrote this novel—there is a redemption in the fact that this story of incest has been told finally from a female point of view, told so well, and, I believe, for the first time in human history in this depth and completeness. There is also an implicitly forgiving attitude in Morrison towards all her characters. We understand Cholly and Soaphead Church, and I find it impossible to hate them; their actions seem inevitable as Pauline's. The book unfolds with all the necessity of any Greek tragedy,[7] but only because the reader's compassion is aroused. No one is indicted for Pecola's destruction, but then in another way we all are. If no one is guilty, there is no scapegoat; the vision becomes more akin to the ancient Necessity, the bleak, irrevocable, futile-to-resist, faceless impingement of an inescapable destiny.

Notes

4. Two sources develop the idea that the mother–daughter dyad is the symbol of futurity, promise, and hope for our humanity. The Demeter–Persephone godhead of the Eleusinian mysteries offers its initiates knowledge of their own immortality through knowledge of these goddesses. C. G. Jung and C. Kerenyi, *Essays on a Science of Mythology: The Myth of the Divine Child and the Mysteries of Eleusis* (Princeton: Princeton University Press, 1949): C. Kerenyi, *Eleusis: Archetypal Image of Mother and Daughter* (New York: Schocken, 1967). The best recent work of mother–daughter imagery is by Estella Lauter in *Feminist Archetypal Theory: Interdisciplinary Re-Visions of Jungian Thought*, ed. Estella Lauter and Carol Schreier Rupprecht (Knoxville: University of Tennessee Press, 1986), pp. 50–62.

7. Morrison herself mentions her studies of the classics in connection with her tragic inclinations, and I think she must have known the ancient conceptions of the Nemesis/Necessity that she so powerfully invokes; "The Language Must Not Sweat," *New Republic* 18 (March 21, 1981): p. 28.

TRUDIER HARRIS ON
LORAIN, OHIO: A WASTELAND

The cultural beliefs that inform the storytelling in *The Bluest Eye* are manifested in a reversal of cultural health for black people, an acquiescence to destructive myths. Morrison creates an environment and a landscape in which infertility is the norm, where values with the potential to sustain have been reversed or perverted, and where few individuals have the key for transcending their inertia. Her depiction of the cycle of seasons without growth, from autumn to summer, evoke, in their mythological implications, comparisons to the legend of the Fisher King and to the world T. S. Eliot creates in *The Waste Land*. The novel is a ritualized exploration of the dissolution of culture and the need for an attendant rite of affirmation. How can the society be saved from itself? What hero, heroine, or heroic change of mind will effect its repair? But Morrison also accomplishes more than these surface comparisons; by setting her novel in a black community, and showing the superimposition of external values upon it, she emphasizes even more the need for rites of renewal, for rebirth from within the community as well as outside of it. The strands of tradition that she fuses in the novel enable Morrison to enrich her story line, to show the peculiarities of her characters, and to connect them to the larger human community.

In Eliot's wasteland, people engage in sex without sharing, indeed without even a minimal concern for their partners; money is valued above all else; there is a meaninglessness in human interactions; and a general malaise exists in which abortions are preferable to delivery, infidelity is common, and culture has collapsed into bar hopping. In Morrison's world, marriage becomes, for most of the characters, an escape from their humdrum previous existences; sex is economic (for the prostitutes), pristine (for the likes of Geraldine and Soaphead Church), or degenerative (for Pauline); change, though constant, does not bring improvement in people's lives; and potentially sustaining values (love, morality, belief in God) have been destroyed by the very institutions that should perpetuate them (church and family). Though Claudia's family provides an oasis in the desert of mythological infertility in the novel, Morrison's world is primarily one in which stagnation is the norm, and where the pursuit of values alien to one's culture ultimately leads to destruction. The seasons of infertility become a metaphor for a larger condition that wears away at the very foundation of the society.[9]

Morrison's choice of the story of Dick and Jane, their mother, father, dog, and cat as the comparative connection for a tale of a little black girl who desperately wants blue eyes makes clear, initially, the listlessness so characteristic of middle-class existence. The outer shell of that myth of perfection might be enviable—a house, a nuclear family, no economic worries, pets, a smiling response to life—but there is a patterned sameness to it that eliminates spontaneity and guarantees a duplication millions of times over. The absence of individuality in the pattern becomes its own kind of inertia and infertility; the mold resists reshaping; those who would aspire to it must reshape themselves to fit the already established pattern. . . .

The middle-class status itself becomes a monster for what it represents, not for what it offers, for certainly there is nothing intrinsically negative in a desire for self-improvement. On the path to this kind of self-improvement, however, individuals must give up too much of themselves in order to view the world from a particular—usually condescending—perspective, as Morrison so vividly depicts in the character of Geraldine. Middle-classness makes her untouchable, closeted, disdainful of the very roots she has used to grow her new status. The individual components of the image are subsumed under the total representation, the "I am better than you because I have it made" attitude that Geraldine conveys to Pecola and that we can imagine her many twin sisters conveying to other unattractive little black girls who mistakenly intrude upon their sacred grounds.

Cleanliness to the point of blandness, houses made into artifacts rather than comfortable abodes, and children who become possessions to be pointed out are just a few of the pitfalls of the middle-class status Morrison depicts; if there are any virtues in being middle class, she does not emphasize them. She is consistently intolerant of those who allow themselves to fit the mold, who allow individuality to be consumed by their notions of progress. Their status becomes another of the wedges splintering the community into almost unsalvageable pieces. As Pecola finds her way through the splinters, she can only reap cuts and bruises, not a pattern for healthy growth.

In Morrison's world, the working-class family has failed in its ability to nurture just as surely as the middle-class family has failed because of its insipidity. A contrasting look at the Breedloves and Geraldine and her family will illustrate the point. Cholly and Pauline probably started out with the usual high hopes and prospects of any newly married couple—having children, acquiring property, becoming respectable citizens. But there are problems stemming from what each spouse brings to the marriage. . . .

By the time Sammy and Pecola are born . . . the marriage has deteriorated into a round of fights, moviegoing, and isolation from people who could possibly give them release from their own hatred of each other. Certainly Pauline goes to church, but she has twisted that institution to serve the purposes of her hateful marriage. Thus the home life that should provide the basis of growth turns out to be a prison in which Sammy and Pecola are trapped along with their parents. Family to them is an abstraction, not something that has a tangible, healthy counterpart in the world. Indeed, it is ironic that the Breedlove family is a nuclear one, for they are no more sustaining in their seeming wholeness than a less unified family would be, and perhaps a family of lesser "completeness" would be much more nurturing.

The very notion of family is predicated upon the assumption that the members in the unit accept its raison d'être. And, presumably, if parents set out to have children, there would be a modicum of acceptance for those children. The breakdown of the structure begins with Pauline's rejection of her children because they are, to her mind, ugly. She says of Pecola when she is born: "*Eyes all soft and wet. A cross between a puppy and a dying man. But I knowed she was ugly. Head full of pretty hair, but Lord she was ugly*" (97–98). In this undermining of one of the basic foundations of the family institution, there can be no happy outcome for the Breedloves, for, in rejecting her children, Pauline not only denies them love, but she denies to them the opportunity to see love exhibited; therefore, if they should grow into marriage and children of their own, they will have no basis upon which to show love or nurturing.

Throughout the novel, we see the consequences of the failure to show love in Pecola's reaction to the world. Since she has received only harsh treatment at home, she expects only harsh treatment from the world outside. She is forever crushed into herself in anticipation of rejection, and her belief that she is ugly, combined with the physical fact, ensures that rejection. Her belief provides for a way of acting and reacting that evokes venom in many of the small children she encounters; when they, in their innocent cruelty, see a target willing to be abused, they willingly oblige. And Pecola, believing that they will abuse her, is unconsciously, eternally the victim. The cycle, vicious in its repetitiveness, is one that is too ingrained to be broken. No change can occur because of the failure in the marriage and family structure, and because of society's faulty way of viewing its members.

Notes

9. In Black Women Novelists: *The Development of a Tradition, 1892–1976* (Westport, Conn.: Greenwood Press, 1980), Barbara Christian refers to the seasons, the Dick and Jane primer, and Claudia's voice as the three "structural motifs . . . the building blocks of the book" (143). In her focus on theme and variation on a theme, the "jazz composition" (144) and recurrent "dominant chords" (148) of the novel, she has suggested an additional structural motif for *Sula*—that of jazz composition.

MARC C. CONNER ON EXTREME COMMUNITY

The great truism of Morrison scholarship is that her primary theme is "community."[1] Certainly each novel rigorously engages such issues as what constitutes a community, what function a community serves, what threatens a community, what helps it survive. As Morrison herself has said, "If anything I do, in the way of writing novels (or whatever I write), isn't about the village or the community or about you, then it is not about anything" (Leonard 706). The relationship between the individual and the community is indeed the central concern of Morrison's rich narratives; yet the complexity of this relationship has in many respects gone largely unnoticed. Most readers view Morrison's emphasis on community in an overwhelmingly positive light, seeing the community as nurturing, cohesive, and healing, and the individual's place within that community as one of security and comfort.[2] But in fact the communities depicted throughout Morrison's fiction, from *The Bluest Eye* to *Paradise*, are predatory, vampiric, sterile, cowardly, threatening; and the individual must struggle desperately to survive in the midst of this damaging community—a struggle that is often a losing one, resulting in the fragmentation and destruction of these desperate selves.

Morrison's engagement with the relations between the individual and the community reveals a striking progression. In her early novels, *The Bluest Eye* and *Sula*, the individual and the community are clearly opposed to one another, and the community ruthlessly victimizes the individual, ultimately destroying both Pecola and Sula. The two novels that follow, *Song of Solomon* and *Tar Baby*, work to reconcile the self and society, yet each ultimately fails to accomplish this. For Milkman in *Song of Solomon* and Jadine and Son in *Tar Baby*, the individual and community are brought closer, but still left apart and unreconciled. Yet in *Beloved* Morrison for the first time shows communal concerns and individual quests enabling and completing each other: Sethe's need to come to terms with her past is fulfilled only through the community's exorcism of the haunting presence of that past; and in that exorcism the community's own need to be reconciled with Sethe is fulfilled. This reconciliation is continued in *Jazz*, where the community forms the very voice that tells the tale of reconciliation that dominates the novel; and even *Paradise*, which returns to a community that is predatory and destructive, suggests in its mystical close a possibility of healing and restoration. This progression—from annihilation to regeneration, from victimization to reconciliation—demands an interpretive response that can make sense of the shift in Morrison's narrative strategies and her creative vision. . . .

The Bluest Eye presents the fundamental pattern of Morrison's early novels: an isolated figure, cut off from the community, must undergo a harrowing experience, an ontologically threatening encounter with what is variously described as the unspeakable, the otherworldly, the demonic—that is, the sublime. In the encounter with the sublime, these characters are excluded from a general gathering together of the community in beauty and harmony, and are condemned to fragmentation, psychosis, and death. In *The Bluest Eye*, Pecola Breedlove forms a peculiarly unstable core for the book. Pecola has no specified place, and she floats on the peripheries of the community she longs to enter. When Claudia MacTeer is first informed by her mother that Pecola will be staying with them for a few weeks, she is told simply that "a 'case' was coming—a girl who had no place to go." Pecola has become homeless because her drunken father has destroyed their home, "and everybody, as a result, was outdoors" (17). This fear of being "outdoors" is "the real terror of life," a consuming anxiety about being without a fixed abode, without a house: "if you are outdoors, there is no place to go. . . . Outdoors was the end of something, an irrevocable, physical fact" (17–18). This fear of being homeless, radically unsettled, pervades Morrison's fiction. In *The Bluest Eye*, it defines the community's greatest fear, and also its relation to Pecola. For Pecola herself is constantly outdoors, never able to integrate herself into the community, always left on the peripheries, literally moving from house to house searching for a fixed place of comfort and security.

Pecola's position on the fringe of the black community is evident when she is taunted by a group of boys after school, in what Trudier Harris has described as "a rite of separation" in which "Pecola is given another opportunity to view her status as an outsider" ("Reconnecting Fragments" 72). Particularly painful because her own peers are excluding her, the jeers focus on Pecola's blackness and on her father's nakedness, prefiguring both her eventual rape by her father and also her desire to transform her blackness into what the novel posits as the essence of whiteness, the blond hair and bluest eyes of Shirley Temple. Claudia and Frieda's rescue of Pecola is only temporary, for soon Maureen turns on Pecola with the same taunt about her naked father. Pecola's reaction embodies her desire to vanish, to disappear in the face of a communal rejection she cannot bear: "Pecola tucked her head in—a funny, sad, helpless movement. A kind of hunching of the shoulders, pulling in of the neck, as though she wanted to cover her ears. . . . She seemed to fold into herself, like a pleated wing" (60–61).

This complex relationship between individual and community in *The Bluest Eye* is expressed through the ambiguous symbol of the house. The novel opens with the Dick and Jane primer that promises the idyllic home and family for which Pecola searches throughout the book: "Here is the house. It is green and white. It has a red door. It is very pretty. Here is the family. Mother, Father, Dick, and Jane live in the green-and-white house. They are very happy" (7). But as this chant is repeated in subsequent paragraphs, it becomes a frantic, unpunctuated stream of language without order, suggesting that behind this myth of a comforting, nurturing home lies a reality that is disordered and disrupting.

The house serves as the antidote to the evil of being outdoors, offering shelter and safety: "Knowing that there was such a thing as outdoors bred in us a hunger for property, for ownership. The firm possession of a yard, a porch, a grape arbor" (18). This desire for home is also a desire to curb the excess, the "funkiness," of the characters' lives: careful attention to boundary and limit will guard against the "dreadful funkiness of passion, the funkiness of nature, the funkiness of the wide range of human emotions" (68). The men seek a woman who has curbed her funkiness, for they know that such a woman will keep a house in which they will "feel secure" (68–69). But the home as haven is soon translated into the home as prison: "What they do not know is that this plain brown girl will build her nest stick by stick, make it her own inviolable world, and stand guard over its every plant, weed, and doily, even against him" (69). The house is simultaneously a respite and a jail; like the community, for which it stands as synecdoche, the house seems to promise rest and comfort, but it provides neither, especially for Pecola.

After her house is burned by her father, Pecola is twice attracted to other idyllic houses, only to be thrown out of them. When Pecola enters the home of a middle-class neighbor to see his kitten, she is struck by the order and comfort it offers: "How beautiful, she thought. What a beautiful house." But when the boy becomes sadistic and hurls the cat into the window, his mother immediately blames Pecola for disrupting her ordered home: "'Get out,' she said, her voice quiet. 'You nasty little black bitch. Get out of my house'" (73–75). Pecola, hurt and bewildered, is again turned outdoors as she leaves the house to face the cold wind and falling snow. The second incident occurs at the Fisher house, the white family's home where Pecola's mother, Pauline, works. Pauline is so enchanted by the "beauty, order, cleanliness" of the Fisher house that she "stopped trying to keep her own house," and instead "kept this order, this beauty, for herself, a private world" (100–101). Pauline views the Fisher house as the secure and splendid home that is denied her in her own life; she is unaware of its second aspect as a prison, unaware that the house, as the Fishers themselves say of Pauline, will "'never let her go'" (101). When Pecola comes to this house and nervously knocks a blueberry cobbler onto the kitchen floor, her mother strikes and curses her; while she comforts the Fisher daughter, Pauline shouts to Pecola to "'pick up that wash and *get on out of here*'" (87, emphasis added). Thus Pecola is for the third time thrown outdoors, and the house that—like the community as a whole, like Pecola's mother—promised such comfort and safety is transformed into a place of rage and fear, offering no haven for Pecola but only further confirming her isolation.

In this solitary and rejected state, Pecola wishes for the blue eyes that she feels will guarantee her love and acceptance; instead, she undergoes her father's delirium-induced rape of her. This is Pecola's harrowing experience, her contact with the unspeakable, what the book terms "a wild and forbidden thing" (128). Pecola's earlier efforts to disappear are re-enacted in an emptying-out of her spirit from her body, as "a hollow suck of air in the back of her throat" makes a sound like "the rapid loss of air from a circus balloon" (128). The malevolent aspect of the home is again emphasized here, for, as Madonne Miner points out, "Pecola's rape occurs within her own house, and this fact increases its raw horror" (88). Pecola is destroyed within her very community, and that community not only fails to aid her, they have helped cause her isolation.

Notes

1. It is far more difficult to find Morrison essays that do not mention the community than those that do; but representative examples of community-oriented scholarship include Christian; Cynthia A. Davis; Grant; O'Shaugnessy; Mason, Jr.; Mbalia; and Bjork.

2. Significant exceptions include Rosenberg and Trudier Harris. That both of these essays deal with *The Bluest Eye* suggests that Morrison's critique of community is strongest in this first novel, and becomes more subtle in her subsequent work.

LISA WILLIAMS ON THE ARTIST AS STORYTELLER AND SURVIVOR

In Morrison's first novel, she constructs a duality that exists between Claudia MacTeer, the narrator who defies the hierarchy of domination and submission by nurturing her own life and finding words for grief, and Pecola Breedlove, another little girl who is raped and then silenced by her own internalized self-hatred. As the artist figure in the novel, Claudia affirms that there are melodies in grief and to write and speak of those experiences that have remained unrecorded is to begin to heal the invisible wounds created by silence. Claudia is connected to the oral tradition of her ancestors, which is communicated to her through her mother's songs.[1] Pecola, on the other hand, is the stranger in the wasteland of the North, isolated from both the black and white communities. As a result, Pecola longs for the bluest eyes, believing these white features will help her gain entry to all that has excluded her; and yet ultimately her madness becomes her way of self-protectively imagining an interior world that is immune from both the internal and external manifestations of racism.

Pecola Breedlove [is] invisible to those around [her], and as a result, live[s] outside of language. . . . [She] can only retreat into a world of [her] own creation where [she] can find form for [her] muted anger.[3] Morrison does, however, have Claudia find the words for Pecola's pain. By doubling the mad and self-hating little girl who has been silenced by sexual abuse and internalized racism with the resistant artist storyteller, Morrison examines the very conditions that are necessary for the creation of art. . . .

By singling out a poor black girl, Morrison specifically indicts a society in which race, class, and gender prejudices destroy its most vulnerable members. But since Morrison believes this woundability is present in all girls to some extent, she creates a narrative structure that forces the reader to examine what part she plays in upholding the devastating effects of racism and western notions of beauty. In this way, Morrison's aesthetic takes on a distinctly choral nature in which the reader is forced to participate in the story. . . .

Morrison's lyrical language becomes its own antidote to loss. She explains that "the weight of the novel's inquiry on so delicate and vulnerable a character could smash her and lead readers into the comfort of pitying her rather than into an interrogation of themselves for the smashing. My solution— break the narrative into parts that had to be reassembled by the reader" (211).[4] The seasons quietly and imperceptibly changing, the stirring of fall merging into winter, into spring, that border the chapters of this novel, create many silences the reader must fill in through the painful process of self-examination. As the creator of this text, Morrison's attempts "to shape a silence while breaking it are attempts to transfigure the complexity and wealth of Black-American culture into a language worthy of the culture" (216). By giving form to silence, by voicing what has remained mute and invisible in the lives of black women, Morrison transcends silence through language, and in the process transforms the novel as she reinforces her own identity as a writer who uses words to shatter silence.[5] . . .

Carol Gilligan points out that loss of voice is symptomatic of an absence of a relationship with the external environment, since speaking is dependent on listening and being heard ("Remembering Iphigenia" 153). Pecola retreat[s] into illness and madness because there is a split between [her] inner reality and the external world around [her] that renders [her] invisible. In the chasm between inner and outer worlds, language gets lost and buried.[6] In contrast, Claudia, as the storyteller, has the close bonds of her family, as well as a connection to the land itself, to help sustain her voice.[7] In *The Bluest Eye*, Morrison structures her novel so that the adult Claudia, who looks back on the events of her childhood, tells the story of Pecola's destruction. In the telling, Claudia, as narrator, becomes the voice of the artist who uses language to analyze the effects of internalized racism and affirm her own resistance to self-hatred and white western notions of beauty.

While *The Bluest Eye* centers on the rape of a young black girl by her father, the novel is layered with the many hierarchical layers of domination and submission, and greater and smaller rapes that occur throughout its pages. Pecola's rape and the complete annihilation of her person has a long history that dates back to slavery. . . .

It is precisely this social structure, as it is internalized in the lives of the black community, that Morrison dismantles and exposes through the critical voice of Claudia and an impersonal narrator who appears throughout the novel. . . .

The language of *The Bluest Eye* takes on the up and down cadenced rhythms of mourning in the same way that the seasons bordering each chapter heading move from autumn through winter and back out into summer, as if to document the spiritual dying and subsequent effort to heal that has taken place over the course of these pages. Claudia's childlike voice is interspersed with the knowing adult voice who can look back on the events of her life and begin to interpret them. . . .

As she hears her mother sing of those bad times she's endured, Claudia realizes that "misery colored by the greens and blues in my mother's voice took all of the grief out of the words and left me with a conviction that pain was not only endurable, it was sweet" (26). The ability of her mother to sing of pain, to tell her stories through song, makes Claudia long for hard times without "a thin di-i-ime to my name" (25), as she looks forward "to the delicious time when 'my man' would leave me, when I would 'hate to see that evening sun go down . . . 'cause then I would know 'my man has left this town'" (26).

Through her song, Claudia's mother communicates to her daughter the beauty of the African-American folk tradition of storytelling. By listening and then speaking, Claudia becomes a modern-day griot who affirms, as she participates in storytelling, the culture that the white society would like to destroy. Her positive self-identity is nurtured by her continuing relation to a maternal oral tradition. In addition, by telling her story in language that sings of an eerie beauty in the midst of pain, Claudia confirms that loss has its own melodic, harmonic rhythms that can only be unearthed through the speaker's desire to link her experience with words.

Claudia not only rejects white female beauty, but she declares that she will create a life that is different from what the women in the song experience. She takes the melodies she has learned from song and colors the sadness of her story with the greens and blues of the seasons changing and the earth dying, as she criticizes the desire for blue eyes and the idea that to be male is to be constantly in flight. She affirms that the lyrical nature of her storytelling originates in the melodies of her mother's grief turned into song. She is the voice in the novel that dares to imagine a world where children will be protected, where young girls will not be raped by fathers or fondled by fraudulent preachers. Claudia narrates the story of what happens to those who have been marked as "other," as "ugly," those whose experiences do not exist in any text, whose lives lie far outside the words of the Dick and Jane primers that serve to erase their reality.

As the artist figure who gives form to Pecola's pain, Claudia explains how the Breedloves, in sharp contrast to her own family, lived in a storefront house "because they were poor and black, and they stayed there because they believed they were ugly" (39). It is their belief in their ugliness, more than the reality of their poverty, that paralyzes them. Pecola hides behind her ugliness: "Concealed, veiled, eclipsed—peeping out from behind the shroud very seldom, and then only to yearn for the return of her mask" (31). Pecola becomes a mark; she is the symbol, the depository where the eyes of others render her invisible. "She would never know her beauty. She would only see what there was to see: the eyes of other people" (46–47). . . .

Through the character of Pecola, Morrison warns the black female artist of the obscurity and madness that will befall her if she internalizes the racism that is infecting her surroundings, while through the character of Claudia, Morrison demonstrates the actions the black female artist must take, so she can construct an environment in which she can create. . . .

Although Pecola's rape is linked to her parents' departure from the South, Morrison harshly indicts the larger white society and the immediate family and neighbors that have let Pecola slip self-protectively into madness, for it is in Pecola's destruction that historical and personal loss come together. Unlike her father, Pecola has never had any contact with an older, healing ancestor (Trudier Harris 40). Even though Cholly is deserted by both his mother and father, he is taken in by his Aunt Jimmy and surrounded by a nurturing community of old black women. As a child, listening to their chatter, "the lullaby of grief enveloped him, rocked him, and at last numbed him" (TBE 139); and yet while grief and its melodies soothe him at first, Cholly's failure as a man is that grief ultimately made him devoid of feeling. . . .

Morrison says that "the most masculine act of aggression becomes feminized in my language, 'passive,' and I think more accurately repellent when deprived of the male glamour of shame, rape is (or once was) routinely given" (Afterword TBE 215). Rape, too, is rewritten in Morrison's language since she does not want to tell the story of male shame, which is only romanticized by the culture. By describing Cholly in sympathetic terms, she makes his aggressive act all the more violent and insidious.[14] Even as she silences Pecola by telling the rape scene from Cholly's point of view, Morrison writes Pecola's experience into literature since it is Pecola's muted scream that lies beyond the pages where Dick, Jane, Mother, and Father live happily ever after in their white world.[15]

Pecola becomes the maimed grotesque flailing without words. The only sound she can make during the rape is "the hollow suck of air in the back of her throat. Like the rapid loss of air from a circus balloon" (163). Pecola descends naturally into madness where she can finally hallucinate a self she can see. . . .

Pecola's madness can also be seen as part of a wish to heal since she is finally able to construct a self, even if it is out of the fragmented shards of consciousness reflected in her birdlike movements among the garbage and refuse of both the black and white communities that have excluded her.[16] Left to have imaginary conversations with herself, Pecola becomes "a winged, but grounded bird, intent on the blue void it could not reach—could not even see—but which filled the valleys of her mind" (TBE qtd. in Miner 181). As the narrator, it is Claudia who finds words for the pain the nightingale cannot voice, the sounds the severed tongue would like to make. Claudia, like Procne, becomes the loyal sister who will avenge Pecola's destruction by telling of it. The lyrical language of this novel becomes the song the nightingale longs to sing.

Claudia does not have to step into madness in order to create a life that can transcend the self-hatred that gnaws away at Pecola and Pauline Breedlove. She can participate in the creative act of storytelling and maintain a positive self-image precisely because she has been raised in a family that has not severed their ties with their ancestors. In contrast, Pecola expresses the loss of the migrant, the uprooted, who does not even know her past. If Morrison's intention is to "shape a silence while breaking it" (Afterword TBE 216), then Pecola's madness reflects the fragmentation of this broken silence, while Claudia's storytelling is her effort to give it a shape that can transform loss into language.

Notes

1. Gay Wilentz aptly notes, "For African and African-American women writers, generational and cultural continuity—"to look back through our mothers" is seen as a woman's domain. Orature and, consequently, literature are part of many women's daily struggle to communicate, converse, and pass on values to their own and other children, and one another" (*Binding Cultures: Black Women Writers in Africa and the Diaspora* xiv).

3. bell hooks notes: "Madness, not just physical abuse, was the punishment for too much talk if you were female" (*Talking Back* 7).

4. Shelley Wong sees that Morrison's narrative practice involves a two-fold process, "the practice of taking apart and then pouring back together to form the ground of a new order of signification" ("Transgression as Poesis in *The Bluest Eye*" 472).

5. See Audre Lorde, "The Transformation of Silence into Language and Action," for an eloquent discussion of the relationship between healing, writing, and breaking silence (*Sister Outsider* 40–44).

6. Daniel N. Stern maintains "that the very process of learning to speak is recast in terms of forming shared experiences, of re-establishing the 'personal order,' of creating a new type of 'being-with' between adult and child" (205). Both Rachel and Pecola suffer from the absence of close familial bonds.

7. Barbara Christian aptly notes, "Mrs. MacTeer and her circle of friends maintain their strong woman ties as well as an equally strong sense of family. As they absorb the different cycle of seasons that they now experience, they begin to see the town as their town. As a result, one of their daughters, Claudia, is able to tell us the story of Pecola Breedlove's tragedy and is able to wrest understanding rather than waste out of this new land" (*Black Feminist Criticism* 49).

14. According to Philip Page, "Cholly Breedlove suffers almost the same silence as Pecola" (180).

15. Jane S. Bakerman aptly notes, "For Pecola, the healthy sexual encounter symbolizing initiation into the adult world is forbidden, for when someone does see her as lovable, it is her father, and he rapes her" (547).

16. bell hooks notes: "And many of us are daily entering the realm of the insane. Like Pecola, in Toni Morrison's *The Bluest Eye*, black folks turn away from reality because the pain of awareness is so great. Yet it is only by becoming more fully aware that we begin to see clearly" (*Black Looks* 6).

EVELYN JAFFE SCHREIBER ON DOUBLE CONSCIOUSNESS

In *The Bluest Eye*, the voices of marginalized people merge through a double-voiced text. That is, through the dominant social discourse, the emergent culture appears in its reenactment of and resistance to the status quo. The text's creation of double-consciousness exemplifies the struggle for subject status by black Americans, confirming the detrimental effects from the internalization of a negative self-concept.

Confined by white, patriarchal definitions of the self, black characters both incorporate (that is, perform as whites) and reject (through resignation to their unalterable skin color and designation as other) these restrictions. With no means to obtain a positive self-reflection, these characters must confront the gaze that socially constructs them as objects. . . .

Du Bois elaborates the quandary of objectifying double-consciousness in the development of American blacks as follows: "From the double life every American Negro must live, as a Negro and as an American . . . must arise a painful self-consciousness, an almost morbid sense of personality and a moral hesitancy which is fatal to self-confidence. . . . The price of culture is a Lie" (148). *The Bluest Eye* presents the magnitude of this lie and the huge price it extracts through a double-voiced text that delineates white parameters of beauty and behavior and the black reaction to them. Michael Awkward describes how the narrative events of *The Bluest Eye* . . . portray double consciousness as a constant and, for Pecola at least, a permanently debilitating state (58). . . .

The Bluest Eye utilizes double-consciousness to expose the other in the self, contrasting black social immobility with black psychic development. The text reenacts the white constructions of beauty, order, and family to illustrate how the imposition of these standards on blacks prevents the development of a black identity based on African American cultural ritual. As a result, white constructions confine black consciousness. The text reenacts white values, only to deconstruct them and shatter their viability. The balancing of the "normal" (American cultural standards) with the abnormal (negative actions attributed to others) pervades the novel, mirroring the web of double-consciousness inherent in black identity. Morrison's text immediately voices the tragic outcome of the story—the rape of Pecola Breedlove by her father Cholly and the death of her subsequent baby—information Pecola's community would rather bury or repress. . . . By presenting black consciousness as the gaze of the Other, Morrison's novel illustrates the ever-present threat to subjectivity by objectification.

Morrison's text exposes the destructive results of sustaining desire at another's expense by making both white and black communities responsible for the Breedlove tragedy. *The Bluest Eye* examines the destructiveness of socially constructed identity and, particularly, the black individual's battle to define the self. By opening with text from the Dick and Jane primers commonplace to both black and white American students, the text illustrates how the American educational system dispenses expected standards. Presenting the ideal of the American family—a happy unit of mother, father, children, cat, and dog who live in a pretty green-and-white house—this familiar discourse creates a safe territory. However, Morrison's text immediately undercuts this security by repeating the passage, first without punctuation, then again without spacing:

Here is the house. It is green and white. It has a red door.
. . . Here is the house it is green and white it has a red floor.
. . . Hereisthehouseitisgreenandwhiteithasareddoor. (3–4)

Suddenly, the known becomes unknown, the stable becomes rocky. This passage juxtaposes the American standard of normal family life—what Americans internalize—with the collapse of that standard as accessible to all.[3] Claudia confirms this point when she describes her house as old, cold, and green," in contrast to the ideal image (10). . . .

The story begins with the juxtaposition of opposites: "Nuns go by as quiet as lust, and drunken men with sober eyes sing in the lobby of the Greek hotel" (9).[4] Nuns/lust, drunk/sober; these polarities set up what Patricia Hill Collins calls the "outsiders within" condition (S26). Claudia's white neighbor Rosemary taunts her and her sister with their outsider status as she sits in her family's car and

rolls down the window to tell my sister Frieda and me that we can't come in. We stare at her, wanting her bread, but more than that wanting to poke the arrogance out of her eyes and smash the pride of ownership that curls her chewing mouth. When she comes out of the car we will beat her up, make red marks on her white skin. (9) . . .

The girls internalize their place in the social world through these responses to daily encounters. When Claudia is sick and her mother scolds her, her "mother's anger humiliates me; her words chafe my cheeks, and I am crying. I do not know that she is not angry at me, but at my sickness" (11). The anger is directed at the despised other, at what injures and cannot be changed, and her mother finds comfort by singing the blues. In their unresponsive world, the girls wonder about being worthy of love. Mrs. MacTeer's reassuring care of Pecola at the onset of her menses fails to erase Pecola's fears about being loved. From her constant position as rejected other, Pecola wonders, "how do you get somebody to love you?" (32). Pecola's model for love has been her bickering parents, leading her to believe that love is "[c]hoking sounds [Cholly] and silence [Pauline]" (57). Claudia herself has yet to find the answer and can provide no solace for Pecola, admitting that she "didn't know" (32). Both girls acknowledge the unloved black body in a culture that provides nothing to reflect this black body as lovable. . . .

This desire to evade the real and achieve an imagined completeness and place in the dominant social order appears in the text's description of black

girls [who] live in quiet black neighborhoods where everybody is gainfully employed. Where there are porch swings hanging from chains. . . . They go to land-grant colleges, normal schools, and learn how to do the white man's work with refinement: home economics to prepare his food; teacher education to instruct black children in obedience. . . . [They learn] how to behave . . . how to get rid of the funkiness. The dreadful funkiness of passion, the funkiness of nature, the funkiness of the wide range of human emotions. (82–83)

These women attempt to erase all sense of otherness from their lives and to avoid situations that will reveal themselves in the gaze of the Other. Their identification with the dominant culture leads to deidealization. In their desire to copy white society, they deny any uniqueness of black identity. Trudier Harris describes how this "straitjacketing pattern" denies "the spontaneity of black life-styles . . . [and] reflects a self-hatred" (*Fiction* 29).

In *The Bluest Eye*, Geraldine so restricts her son's playmates and activities that he develops a sadistic mean streak. He delights in torturing Pecola and brutally kills his cat. Pecola, initially soothed by the black cat's blue eyes, sees her own negated self in them when it dies, "its blue eyes closed, leaving only an empty, black, and helpless face" (91). Despite efforts to gain subject status through identification with the dominant social order, blacks remain other, present only in absence, in what they lack. . . .

Dependence on victimization or the objectifying of others for subjectivity constantly threatens the subject position, and it is from this precarious position that the community continues to reject and avoid Pecola. Claudia discovers that her black community and the white society that molds it are "bad for certain kinds of flowers" and that "the victim had no right to live" (206). Thus, although "the primary function of the black community [i]s that of protecting its members," Pecola's community fails her (Harding and Martin 89). Cormier-Hamilton summarizes that "without the strength of love for one's cultural identity, vulnerable members of minorities are in real danger of being starved by both black and white environments" (122). In her madness, Pecola escapes to a world where she is "beautiful," a world of pure imaginary wholeness. In her psychotic state. Pecola obtains the object of her desire, the blue eyes. Her fantasy separates her from how others treat her, thereby succeeding in protecting her from pain.

In her "Afterword" to *The Bluest Eye*, Morrison states that she asked, why was racial beauty

> not . . . taken for granted within the community? Why did it need wide public articulation to exist? . . . The assertion of racial beauty was not a reaction to the self-mocking, humorous critique of cultural/racial foibles common in

all groups, but against the damaging internalization of assumptions of immutable inferiority originating in an outside gaze. (210)

Yet recognition of that damaging gaze ultimately provides a source of agency. Morrison alludes to this capability when she continues by saying that in writing this novel, there was a problem with "language. Holding the despising glance while sabotaging it was difficult. The novel tried to hit the raw nerve of racial self-contempt, expose it, then soothe it not with narcotics but with language that replicated the agency I discovered in my first experience of beauty" (211). The ability to sabotage the gaze—to reverse that gaze to gain a subject position—is the first step in altering subjectivity. While characters in *The Bluest Eye* largely fail to develop that ability, some characters in *Song of Solomon* succeed in that direction. The reenactment of and resistance to the dominant culture embedded in *The Bluest Eye* leads to the emergent black voice in *Song of Solomon*, where encounters with the gaze of the Other can move the racialized other from object to subject.

Notes
3. John N. Duvall notes that the "dysfunction of the nuclear family is particularly freighted for Morrison, since she sees African-Americans who attempt to live within its frame as inauthentically trying to assimilate to the values of white culture" ("Toni Morrison" 11).

4. I would like to thank Toni Morrison for correcting my text to reflect the language of her manuscript, rather than the error of her publisher in the printed text.

LUCILLE P. FULTZ ON BLACK FEMALE PAIN

In *The Bluest Eye*, Morrison depicts several sources of black women's pain: old age, death, and the collective memories of suffering and triumph, middle age and thwarted desires, and childhood with its concomitant hurts. Just as Claudia and the omniscient narrator have primary responsibility to recount scenes of suffering, so do other characters provide direct access to their troubled interior worlds. The novel also records black women's discrete and collective experiences that negatively impact their lives. Aunt Jimmy's illness and death provide opportunities for women to reiterate their lived experiences as objects of the community's power and subjection. These women, who seem to have "edge[d] into life from the back door. Becoming . . ."with only one group from whom they do not have to take orders—their children (109), offer us some insights into familial and personal relationships through the conflation of black women's pain with Aunt Jimmy's illness, or with what M'Dear, the "competent midwife" and "decisive diagnostician," terms a "cold in [her] womb" (108). The literal and metaphorical coalesce in Aunt Jimmy's womb: it is both the repository of physical life and the symbolic site of femaleness; it is at once the organ of fertility and the sign of loss and separation—the source of connection and disconnection between the mother and child. The womb can bear fruit and signal barrenness. So the cold in Aunt Jimmy's womb accrues polysemy as it signals Aunt Jimmy's death and the beginning of Cholly's independence.

After M'Dear's pronouncement and departure, Aunt Jimmy is visited by two other friends, Miss Alice and Mrs. Gaines, whose "voices blended into a threnody of nostalgia about pain. Rising and falling, complex in harmony, uncertain in pitch, but constant in the recitative of pain" (109). Aunt Jimmy's deathbed becomes the site of memory and loss—a moment for recollection and release. The three women recite a condensed history of pain that includes perseverance and a necessary distinction between what *was* and what *is*. The element of triumph stems from their having endured the miseries of their youth and middle age: "They hugged the memories of illness to their bosoms . . . licked their lips and clucked their tongues in fond remembrance of pains they had endured" (109). Their pain is expressed in a pre-eulogy for Aunt Jimmy and a shared knowledge that constitutes both litany and praisesong: "childbirth, rheumatism, croup, sprains, backaches, piles. All of the bruises they had collected from moving about the earth—harvesting, cleaning, hoisting, pitching, stooping, kneeling, picking—always with young ones underfoot" (109). The narrator hastens to add details that render this pain race and gender specific. These women have risen above the humiliations and pain, even though "everybody in the world was in a position to give them orders. White women said, 'Do this.' White children said, 'Give me that.' White men said, 'Come here.' Black men said, 'Lay down.' . . . When white men beat their men, they [the women] cleaned up the blood and went home to receive abuse from the victim" (109–10). The violence these women have endured from their own men invites our scrutiny of the double bind in which African American women often find themselves: objects of male abuse and surrogates for white men who go unpunished by their victims—black men.

Aunt Jimmy's death opens a space for black women to reflect on their lives, and it is an occasion to assess black women's lives, a process the narrator encapsulates in one sentence: "The lives of these old black women were synthesized in their eyes—a purée of tragedy and humor, wickedness and serenity, truth and fantasy" (110). The passage stresses both suffering and pleasure. Instead of sentimentalizing their pain, the narrator valorizes their strength and perseverance. Margaret Wilkerson notes that this description "implies the rise and fall of the women's voices and the nuances of their dialogue." Wilkerson hears in "the tone of their speech . . . the ritual of the wake," which she terms "a muted prelude to the joy of the funeral banquet that follows" (187). After Aunt Jimmy's interment, the narrator comments that "there was grief over the waste of life, the stunned wonder at the ways of God, and the restoration of nature in the graveyard" (113). The living are left with the pain and emptiness of death. The litany concludes with the acceptance of suffering and death and the continuation of life. For Aunt Jimmy's female friends, one solution to pain and suffering is living with the knowledge of both and holding on in spite of them. The narrator's summation of this illuminating moment—"Thus the banquet [at the home of the deceased is] the exultation, the harmony, the acceptance of physical frailty, joy in the termination of misery. Laughter, relief, a steep hunger for food" (113)—suggests that the desire to live overwhelms the shadow of death.

Aunt Jimmy's narrative, part of Pauline's and Pecola's histories by way of Charlie Breedlove's, is located in the South, while Geraldine's narrative, deeply rooted in her Southern past, is set in the North. The narratives establish a tenuous dichotomy, one that marks superficial differences because at the core Geraldine cannot escape the world of pain many other black women have known, her well-groomed body and comfortable house notwithstanding. In contrast to Aunt Jimmy's narrative that takes place in "spring," Geraldine's narrative is set in winter. She is, by implication, associated with decay and deadness. She is depicted as part of a large category of women who share her vision and sensibility, women who "go to land-grant colleges, normal schools, and learn," among other things, "how to behave . . . how to get rid of the funkiness. The dread funkiness of passion, the funkiness of nature, the funkiness of the wide range of human emotions" (68). While the women at Aunt Jimmy's wake recognize and claim the sources of their pain, Geraldine denies the reality of her condition through her obsessive neatness, a defense against her psychic tension. This denial transmutes to internalized anguish and repressed anger over her blackness as a mark of limitation and confinement to a black existence The weight of this reality causes Geraldine to project her internal struggles with blackness onto her son and onto Pecola, who represents what Madonne M. Miner describes as "a series of signs, symbolic configuration"—a composite of all the negative baggage Geraldine associates with blackness—"everything ugly, dirty and degrading" (185).

Geraldine's appropriation of bourgeois values—or what Ann Cook, at the time, called "white values in black face" (149)—masks the anger and anguish associated with her blackness, a condition she tries to transcend by keeping a well-groomed son and a spotless house, not unlike Helene Wright's "oppressive neatness" and "curdled scorn" of Sula (Sula 19).[5] Geraldine's behavior also belies the exterior manifestations of what Pecola sees as a "pretty milk-brown lady in the pretty gold-and-green house" (76). What Pecola does not recognize is, as Gurleen Grewal remarks, that Geraldine's "virtuous stability is built upon the repression of her embodied blackness" (29). Pecola's surprise and confusion over Geraldine's outburst result from the contradiction between Geraldine's appearance and her actions. It is evident from her unprovoked verbal flailing at Pecola that Geraldine is reacting to something deep within herself—repressed anger and frustration prompted by racism that compel her to suffer overtly as a black woman while she exists internally as a white woman. Pecola sees Geraldine's exteriority in the interior of her house, but we see beyond Pecola's vision into Geraldine's lifelong suffering, as well as into Pecola's unarticulated desire as she gazes at "the blue eyes in the black face" of Geraldine's cat (*Bluest* 75). Pecola is more than mesmerized by the cat's blue eyes; she sees in them the possibility for her wish fulfillment.

Note

5. Freud, in "A Case of Hysteria," describes this condition as "housewife's psychosis" rather than "obsessive neurosis" since the women afflicted with the malady have no "insight into their illness." He uses Dora's description of her mother's preoccupation with house chores as an example, one that, in some respects, describes Geraldine, Pauline, and Helene Wright. Dora's mother "had no understanding of her children's more active interests, and was occupied all day long in cleaning the house with its furniture and in utensils and in keeping them clean—to such an extent as to make it impossible to use or enjoy them" (10). Consider Nel Wright, who "regarded the oppressive neatness of her home with dread" (*Sula* 19).

DOREATHA DRUMMOND MBALIA
ON CLASS VERSUS RACE AS A
CAUSE OF BLACK OPPRESSION

In *The Bluest Eye*, Toni Morrison's emphasis is on racism, specifically, she investigates the effects of the beauty standards of the dominant culture on the self-image of the African female adolescent. The role of class, the primary form of exploitation experienced by African people that will become the focus of later works, is only relevant insofar as it exacerbates that self-image. Of the three main characters—all African female adolescents—it is Pecola Breedlove who is the primary focus. It is she who is most affected by the dominant culture's beauty standards because it is she who is the poorest and, consequently, the most vulnerable. Thus, even with this early work, Morrison is conscious of the role economics plays in the African's having a wholesome self-image. For it is the Breedloves' fight for survival that weakens the family structure and makes the family members more vulnerable to the propaganda of the dominant culture. Still, it is clear that in *The Bluest Eye* Morrison regards racism as the African's primary obstacle. Describing the Breedloves, she writes: "Although their poverty was traditional and stultifying, it was not unique. But their ugliness was unique."[1] This comment demonstrates that in the late 1960s, when this novel was written, Morrison's level of consciousness about the primary cause of the nature of the African's oppression in the United States as well as in the rest of the world was considerably weak, for she not only subordinates the role of economics to racism, but also neglects to show a causal relationship between them, that an exploitative economic system gives rise to racist ideology. . . .

Although Morrison clearly and correctly understands that the concept of beauty is a learned one—Claudia MacTeer learns to love the big, blue-eyed baby doll she is given for Christmas; Maureen Peal learns she is beautiful from the propaganda of the dominant society as well as from the African adult world; and Pauline Breedlove learns from the silver screen that every face must be assigned some category on the scale of absolute beauty—Morrison does not yet understand that this concept will change depending on the racial makeup of the dominant class. That is, her immature class consciousness at this point in her writing career precludes her understanding of three important facts: first, that the ruling class, whether of European, African, or Asian descent, possesses the major instruments of economic production and distribution as well as the means of establishing its sociocultural dominance (i.e., all forms of media including books, billboards, and movies);

second, that possessing such means, the ruling class uses and promotes its own image as a measurement of beauty for the entire society; and third, that the success of this promotion ensures the continual dominance of this ruling class.

Although her class analysis is immature at this point, Morrison is at least conscious of a limited role that economics plays in the exploitation of African people. For example, Morrison begins *The Bluest Eye* with a page and a half of one passage repeated in three different ways. Each of the passages reflects the three primary families in the novel: the Dick-Jane primary reader family, the MacTeer family, and the Breedlove family. The first family is symbolic of the ruling class; it is an economically stable family. Both the MacTeers and the Breedloves symbolize the exploited class although the Breedloves are less economically stable than the MacTeers. In fact, the spacing of the passages reflects the varying economic levels of these families. Although the MacTeers are poor, the father works and provides some shelter, food, and clothing for the economic survival of the family. On the other hand, the Breedloves are dirt poor, and it is the extent of their poverty that strips them of their sense of human worth and leaves them more vulnerable to the cultural propaganda of the ruling class. Their house, significantly a rundown, abandoned store, reflects no stability. The family members come and go like store patrons, having no sense of family love and unity. That Morrison takes the time to describe and explain the poor economic conditions of the Breedlove family, and the effects of these conditions on it, reflects her awareness of the class question. At least she informs the reader that the MacTeers and Breedloves do not suffer simply because of racism, but because of poverty as well.

Additionally, Morrison reveals her class consciousness by exploring the intraracial prejudices caused by petty bourgeois Africans, those who aspire for the same goals and aspirations of the ruling class. In *The Bluest Eye*, she creates three "minor" African families who, because they benefit economically, politically, and/or socially from the exploitation of their own people, disassociate themselves from poor Africans and associate themselves with the ruling class.

One such family is the Peals. Although the reader is introduced to only one member of this family, Maureen, her appearance, behavioral patterns, and remarks about the nature of her family's "business" offer sufficient glimpses of the Peals to reflect their class interests. Physically, Maureen looks and dresses like a little European-American girl, the storybook Jane or the child actress Shirley Temple. Her hairstyle, "long brown hair braided into two lynch ropes that hung down her back" resembles that of little European girls. In fact, the description of her hair as lynch ropes clearly associates her with the African's oppressors.[4] Her "high-yellow" complexion and her clothes make this association even more pronounced. She wears "Kelly-green knee socks," "lemon-drop sweaters," "brown velvet coat trimmed in white rabbit fur, and a matching muff."[5]

Socially, Maureen's behavior patterns reflect the way in which some within the dominant class relate to poor African people. She pities Pecola when she is humiliated by Bay Boy and Junie Bug, and she humors Claudia by speaking to her on one occasion after neglecting her on many others. Economically, the Peal family appears to make money by exploiting the race issue. They initiate suits against European-American establishments (e.g., Isaley's ice cream store in Akron) that refuse to serve Africans. Although, according to Maureen, her "family does it all the time,"[6] apparently these suits are benefitting financially no other African family but the Peals. . . .

By disassociating itself from the African community, the second family—Geraldine, Louis, and Louis Junior—also reflects ruling class aspirations. The family members consider themselves to be *colored*, a term that for them signifies some nebulous group of Africans who are neither European nor African: "Colored people were neat and quiet; niggers were dirty and loud."[9] So Louis Jr. plays with European-American children; his hair is cut short to deemphasize its woolliness; his skin is continually lotioned to keep him from revealing his ashy Africanness. When Geraldine sees Pecola, she is reminded of everything she has sought to escape—everything associated with the poor, struggling African masses: their physical appearance, their behavioral patterns, their lifestyle, and their speech patterns. Her calling Pecola, a little girl of ten, a "nasty little black bitch" and commanding her to "get out of my house" illustrate the extent of Geraldine's isolation from her people and her association with her oppressors. Perhaps even more significant is the fact that she showers love on her black cat, but not her "black" son. Clearly, for her, the blue eyes of the cat make it easier to love the animal than her own son. All in all, her thoughts, words, and actions parrot those of the ruing class.

The third family, the Elihue Micah Whitcombs, are so obsessed with the physical appearance of Europeans that they jeopardize their mental stability by intermarrying to maintain some semblance of whiteness. . . . Not only do the Whitcombs strive for the "whiteness" of the ruling class, but they imitate the exploitive nature of this class as well; they exploit their own people, the Africans who live in the West Indies: "That they were corrupt in public and private practice, both lecherous and lascivious, was considered their noble right."[12]

Clearly, Morrison's class consciousness, however weak, is reflected in her condemnation of these families who share the class aspirations of their oppressors. All suffer from what Kwame Nkrumah called the crisis of the African personality— Africans so bereft of their own national identity that they exhibit distorted, even psychopathic, behavioral patterns. Morrison is certainly aware of this crisis, for in this work as in later ones, she harshly criticizes those characters who divorce themselves from the African community. In fact, she considers this petty bourgeois sector of the African population the living dead, a buffer group between the ruling and the oppressed classes who are always portrayed as abnormal in some sense. In *The Bluest Eye*, Geraldine lavishes love on her black cat, but withholds it from her son; the Whitcombs become a family of morons and perverts. Quite appropriately, Elihue is donned Soaphead Wilson by the community for he is a pervert who is incapable of healthy love. Instead, he loves worn things and little girls; Pecola is both worn (loss of virginity) and a little girl.

Morrison's characterization of these three "minor" families— the Peals, the "Geraldines," and the Whitcombs—certainly substantiates the premise that she does possess some class consciousness even in this first novel. However, that these are not major families in the novel indicates that her class consciousness is decidedly weak. Moreover, even though Morrison is conscious of the role class aspirations play in these minor families, she often discusses these aspirations as if they were intraracial prejudices based on skin color rather than class conflicts. That is, her discussions of class conflicts are couched within, and thus overshadowed by, her discussions on racial prejudices. Indeed, it is interesting to note that just as Africans in the United States in the 1960s and early 1970s viewed the primary enemy of African people as "the white man," so does Morrison, writing *The Bluest Eye* in the late 1960s, see the issue as one of European versus African. However, as she continues to think about, write about, and experience the ongoing oppression of African people despite the gains of the Civil Rights Movement, she will become more conscious of the fact that capitalism, not racism, is the African's greatest enemy.

Notes

1. Toni Morrison, *The Bluest Eye* (New York: Washington Square Press, 1970), 24.

4. The Harlem Renaissance poet and novelist, Jean Toomer, made clear this association between the European female's hair and lynching in his short poem, "Portrait in Georgia":

Hair—braided chestnut, coiled like a lyncher's rope,
Eyes—fagots,
Lips—old scars, or the first red blisters,
Breath—the last sweet scent of cane,
And her slim body, white as the ash of black flesh after flame.

Toni Morrison, student of African literature and former English major and teacher, is certainly aware of Toomer's poem. Her point that Maureen Peal's hair resembles lynch ropes is intended to remind the reader of this poem and thus to elicit feelings of apprehension and ugliness rather than beauty.

5. Morrison, *The Bluest Eye*, 53.

6. Ibid., 57.

9. Morrison, *The Bluest Eye*, 71.

12. Ibid., 133.

The Bluest Eye has been given credit for enabling "the explosion of women's writing and speaking about incestuous abuse" that began in the late 1970s (Gwin 67). Critics Doane and Hodges read the novel as groundbreaking because it "made the incest narrative available to many other writers, such as white feminists, who use accounts of incest to articulate a history of subjugation" (331). Morrison's remarks during her appearance on *The Oprah Winfrey Show* (2000) support this aspect of the book's reception: "A lot of white women write to me about *The Bluest Eye because of* the incest, a lot of white females who are interested in the book because of *that*, not the other level of meaning." But without diminishing the importance of the novel to subsequent narratives of incest, Morrison's comment also suggests that she does not see the book as primarily "about" incest. Moreover, the novel itself does not support a particularly feminist understanding of incest. Judith Herman views father–daughter incest as a "consequence of male socialization within the patriarchal family" (56), and she and other psychologists and case workers "have pointed to the 'normality' of the offenders, their families and their lives" (Bell 3). However, Cholly Breedlove, the incestuous father in *The Bluest Eye*, has had no such socialization. The novel represents father–daughter incest as a consequence of the disempowerment of the black male, who because of racism is not able to fulfill the role of father.[9] Morrison uses the incest story not to indict patriarchy, but to expose a system of racial othering in which the father is as much a victim as the daughter."[10] What *The Bluest Eye* does share with a feminist discourse of incest is the idea that incest can produce power rather than bring about social collapse. And because incest is used in *The Bluest Eye* to show how racial hierarchies are established and maintained, the novel also signifies on the earlier representations of incest in the interracial literature that Sollors has described. *The Bluest Eye* rewrites the Southern romance in which incest brings about the social decay and destruction of a "white" family. In it, incest completes the destruction of a black family, while reconstituting a system of white hegemony.

Morrison demonstrates her engagement with the disciplinary power of incest discourse by the way she introduces the incest plot at the beginning of the novel as a site of interpretation, or, more to the point, as a site of misinterpretation. In the italicized preface to the novel, the narrator, Claudia McTeer, now grown up, says,

> Quiet as it's kept, there were no marigolds in the fall of 1941. We thought, at the time, that it was because Pecola was having her father's baby that the marigolds did not grow. A little examination and much less melancholy would have proved to us that our seeds were not the only ones that did not sprout; nobody's did. (5)

In this opening passage, Morrison deflates the explanatory power of the incest taboo and its violation. She signals her readers that they are not to interpret Cholly's rape of his daughter as the primary cause for natural and social dysfunction, or even for the destruction of Pecola herself. In order to interpret Pecola's destruction the novel asks that we understand the relationship between an ideology of white supremacy and a discourse of incest that promotes and maintains that ideology. Claudia makes this connection when she compares her and her sister's act of planting the marigolds to Cholly's act of impregnating his daughter. She says, "We had dropped our seeds in our own little plot of black dirt just as Pecola's father had dropped his seeds in his own plot of black dirt. Our innocence and faith were no more productive than his lust or despair" (5–6). By changing the signification of "black dirt" from a rich, growing medium to a racial slur, Claudia demonstrates how Pecola became the depository not only of her father's seed, but of a racist discourse that equates black skin with moral degeneracy. The community's act of scapegoating Pecola as a racial and moral other functions to maintain notions of white superiority and seriously compromises the "innocence and faith" of the girls wishing to grow flowers in black earth. Metaphorically joining Claudia's act with Cholly's, the narrator suggests the pervasive and unacknowledged damage caused by racism and implicates the larger community in the problem. The secret, signified by the opening phrase, "quiet as it's kept," becomes not the story of incest, which is, after all, known to the community and put to predictable use, but the story of racial self-loathing, a story more problematic and difficult to tell.

The story of racial self-loathing is told through Pecola's quest for blue eyes, a quest that originates in the violation of Pecola's black body by a white gaze. The logic of Pecola's desire is undeniable, born as it is from the daily experience of being told directly and indirectly that her blackness makes her "ugly," unlovable. The white gaze is ubiquitous. It is in Rosemary Villanucci's "fascinated eyes in a dough-white face" (30). It is in the coveted Shirley Temple cup, in the "blue-eyed, yellow-haired, pink-skinned doll[s] that every girl child treasured" (20), and in the Mary Jane candy wrappers. It is in the distaste of the shopkeeper who does not want to touch Pecola's hand (49); in the group of black boys who circle Pecola and chant, "Black e mo. Back e mo. Yadaddsleepsnekked" (65); in the scream of the high yellow girl, Maureen Peal, "I am cute! And you ugly! Black and ugly" (73); in the words of Geraldine, "You nasty little black bitch. Get out of my house" (92). It is in the eyes of Pecola's mother, Pauline, who describes her newborn as "a right smart baby . . . But I knowed she was ugly. Head full of pretty hair, but Lord she was ugly" (126). And it is in the very device Morrison uses to structure the novel: the public school primer, the Dick and Jane Reader, which introduces Pecola to what it means to be part of a "normal" American family, circa 1944.

Metaphorically speaking, Pecola has been raped by "whiteness," long before her father enters her. The great irony of the father–daughter incest is that unlike the previous "rapes," the incest represents not just another violation but also an act of love. The actual incest scene occurs at the end of the chapter describing the father's life and is rendered entirely from the father's point of view. The reader views the father's act not as an assertion of power, but as the culmination of his tortured experiences with love and intimacy—experiences that in many respects parallel his daughter's. Cholly was abandoned from infancy by both of his parents, the grandmother who raises him dies when he is fourteen, his sexual initiation is marked by a humiliating encounter with white hunters who make him "perform" at gun point, and his search for his father ends in brutal rejection. Yet Cholly also falls in love with Pauline, Pecola's mother. Morrison makes it clear that while that relationship has deteriorated into grotesque violent encounters, it originated as a love match. Cholly's rape of his daughter is infused with his memory of the affection and tenderness he felt for Pauline. His motivations are contradictory. In the moments before the rape, as Cholly watches Pecola washing dishes in the kitchen, "the sequence of his emotions [is] revulsion, guilt, pity, then love" (161). "He want[s] to fuck her—tenderly" (163). At the end of the novel, the narrator says that Cholly "was the one who loved [Pecola] enough to touch her. . . . But his touch was fatal" (206). Morrison ironically suggests that Cholly's incestuous act is the one affirmation of her blackness that Pecola experiences. Incest, in this novel, thus both reinforces and exposes the taboo of blackness.

Notes

9. Also see Morrison's discussion of Cholly in her 1977 interview with Jane Bakerman:

> In *The Bluest Eye*, Cholly, Pecola's father, is a broken man drained by poverty and circumstance, so "he might love her in the worst of all possible ways because he can't do this and he can't do that. He can't do it normally, healthily and so on. So it might end up this way [in the rape]. I want here to talk about how painful it is and what the painful consequences are of distortion, of love that isn't fructified, is held in, not expressed." (rpt. in Taylor-Guthrie 41)

10. Minrose Gwin also understands Cholly's rape of Pecola as a consequence of "race and class disempowerment" (75). However, in

Gwin's reading whiteness becomes a metaphor for patriarchy. "We see the force field of whiteness exert itself in the black community. In this sense whiteness becomes the abusive father" (79). She argues that the novel is about the power dynamics of incest, while I am arguing that *The Bluest Eye* is about the power dynamics of racism and the way in which incest is read as a form of social and racial control.

SUSAN NEAL MAYBERRY ON THE IDEAL OF PHYSICAL BEAUTY

In addition to ultraconservative Western attitudes toward sexuality and ownership, two other white male concepts help turn MacTeers into Breedloves and do irreparable damage to the men in black families: the ideal of physical beauty and the concept of romantic love.[8] Morrison asserts that the Breedloves do not live in the storefront simply because of their race and class; they stay there because no one could have convinced them that they are not uniquely ugly. Although close examination reveals no immediate physical reason for this ugliness, readers come to realize that its source lies in the Breedloves' own conviction:

> It was as though some mysterious all-knowing master had given each one a cloak of ugliness to wear, and they had each accepted it without question. The master had said, "You are ugly people." They had looked about themselves and saw nothing to contradict the statement; saw, in fact, support for it leaning at them from every billboard, every movie, every glance. "Yes," they had said, "You are right." And they took the ugliness in their hands, threw it as a mantle over them, and went about the world with it. Dealing with it each according to his way. (39)

Her words couched in the mesmerizing language of the biblical creation story, Morrison's narrator, unquestionably and scathingly, identifies the mysterious "master" as a white male god who looks down on black people and re-creates them according to his own image. She describes the process of the white gaze, which, when absorbed and reflected by black people, becomes de-creative. Using a term that she will refer to again in a 1994 film interview with Bill Moyers as the *master narrative*, Morrison here connects seeing with knowing.

Medieval optics provides a helpful background for the power relations troped in this scene: medieval vision theory credited both the seer and the object of sight as active contributors to the process of vision. According to the long-held theory of extramission inherited from Aristotle and Augustine, the "visual ray, the strongest concentration of the body's animating fire, is projected from the eye to touch its object. In the act of vision viewer and image are connected in a dynamic communication. . . . In the activity of seeing, the life energy of the viewer goes out to and takes the shape of the object contemplated" (Miles 45). Embedded within this process are paradoxes of power and powerlessness, activity and passivity, self and other, emotion and knowledge. Early modern optics replaced this interactive model of vision with the phenomenological aspects of vision, which emphasize objectivity: distance, detachment, spatialization, simultaneity. However, either of these alternative ways of seeing, acknowledged by Evelyn Fox Keller as shaping our assumptions about how we know, reveals that seeing has always been our most powerful metaphor for knowing. It thus influences subject-object, gender, and power relations: white males have traditionally been the seers in American culture; others, especially black males, the seen.

A "high-yellow dream child" introduces Claudia and Frieda to the "white gaze." Blissfully enjoying their senses, cultivating their dirt, and admiring their scars, they can destroy white dolls but cannot dismiss the "honey voices of parents and aunts, the obedience in the eyes of [their] peers, the slippery light in the eyes of [their] teachers when they encountered the Maureen Peals of the world." Only their support for each other allows the sisters to know that Maureen is not worthy of the hatred they feel toward her, that the "*Thing* to fear was the *Thing* that made *her* beautiful, and not [them]" (74). Alone and far more passive than Claudia or Frieda, Pauline indulges her ugliness, introduced to her by white male movie directors. After leaving her people to go up north with Cholly, she escapes the lonesome bleakness of the storefront by giving herself over to the white images flashing on the silver screen in a black theater. There she also reawakens her memory of darkened woods, lonely roads, riverbanks, and gentle knowing eyes, melancholy childhood fantasies in which burgeoning sexuality transforms into sweet yearning, the physical lover into a mysterious Presence. Church spirituals nourish these romantic dreams, joining love and death into desire for the precious male Stranger who will take Pauline's hand and lead her on; a contralto voice captures the dark sweetness Pauline cannot articulate.

Hearing black spirituals and seeing the white silver screen, then, shape Pauline's assumptions about how she knows herself. From what are actually simple pleasures, she learns "all there was to love and all there was to hate." They become her education in romantic love and physical beauty, according to Morrison probably "the most destructive ideas in the history of human thought." Both "originated in envy, thrived in insecurity, and ended in disillusion. In equating physical beauty with virtue, [Pauline] stripped her mind, bound it, and collected self-contempt by the heap. . . . She regarded love as possessive mating, and romance as the goal of the spirit. It would be for her a well-spring from which she would draw the most destructive emotions, deceiving the lover and seeking to imprison the beloved, curtailing freedom in every way" (122).

Note

8. Morrison's oeuvre implies alternatives apart from the accusatory critique of a dominant white male, Western worldview. It suggests that masculine anxiety is not necessarily race specific and that "African American identity constitutes a problem not for black people alone" (Harper xi). Approaching white patriarchal ideals of a "discrete, unified selfhood and the sovereignty of the will" as "dangerous fantasies," she apprehends black manhood as a "discursive construct shaped by words and by generational dialogues about cultural heritage."

Affirming the viability of pluralistic masculinities, she believes men must "acknowledge that traumatic, shameful Otherness" lurking beyond rational control and beneath idealized self-images (Reed 538–39). Utterance of trauma begins the process of transforming the hollow shell of hegemonic masculine identity into a genuine expression of selfhood, which embraces diversity and accepts certain patriarchal practices as useful while rejecting others. The central challenge for Morrison's males involves reimagining themselves as men "whose subjectivity is not bound up in the context of work or the concatenations of the city scape." Wage labor and overstimulation, because bound to hierarchy, lead to exploitation. Rejecting the phenomenology of the twentieth-century drive to become "a thing apart, the Other as power," Morrison defends the importance of collective talent; self-ownership occurs when "men give themselves up to those forces beyond their grasp" (Beavers 68–75). For her, the elusive masculine dream can best he reached by collaboration.

TRACEY L. WALTERS ON MORRISON'S USE OF THE PERSEPHONE MYTH

In *The Bluest Eye*, Morrison appropriates the Persephone and Demeter myth to discuss the sexual and psychological victimization of women. Rape becomes one of the central issues treated in Morrison's narrative. Rape, as Jaffar-Agha concludes, "does not necessarily entail a violent, physical penetration of our bodily integrity. However, it must constitute a violent intrusion into our psyche—an intrusion that transforms us irrevocably and one from which we cannot return" (145). In the novel the white aesthetic violates Pecola's mind and ultimately drives her insane. Pecola is raped twice: first, by the dominant culture's ideology of whiteness that denigrates Blackness and destroys her identity, and later, by her father. Rape and sexual molestation is a prevailing theme in classical mythology. Men whose motivations are capricious routinely rape female characters. Ovid's *Metamorphoses* recounts numerous stories of women who are violated by men who desire them. In today's world Apollo's pursuit of Daphne would be classified as sexual harassment (Daphne literally runs for her life to escape from Apollo's sexual advances). In another case Philomela is unable to defend herself from Tereus' brutal attack.

In addition to raping her Tereus also mutilates her tongue. Jove is perhaps the biggest predator of women's sexuality. A number of mythical stories in Ovid's metamorphosis recount his routine sexual abuse of women like Io, Callisto, and Europa. When *The Bluest Eye* was published it became part of an emerging discourse on sexual violence against women. The Black Arts movement and women's rights movements gave Black women greater publishing opportunities. More than ever before, Black women wrote about incest, rape, insanity, and Black male abuse of Black women. The subject of rape in particular became an important issue tackled by socially conscious Black women writers. . . . The novels, articles, and social activism involving rape discourse attest to the significance of the mythical story for contemporary audiences: rape and violence against women continue to plague women's lives.

Like other women in this study Morrison's goal is to present classical myth from the Black female perspective. So, whereas in the archetypal narrative Persephone's victimization is a result of her gender inferiority—Hades is able to abduct her because she is a helpless female—with Morrison's Persephone figure the intersecting oppressions of race, class, and gender contribute to her subversion. As a poor, Black child, Pecola lives in the margins of society. Pecola is an invisible stain on society's conscience; no one saves Pecola because, like Pepita of Brooks's "In the Mecca," no one cares about her well-being. And unlike the mythic Persephone or Pepita, Pecola has no Demeter figure to rescue her. Similar to "In the Mecca," Morrison's rendition of the Persephone–Demeter myth rewrites the Homeric and Ovidian fairytale ending because in the real world, poor, Black girls who are kidnapped and raped seldom return home. . . .

Morrison's reenactment of the Persephone–Demeter myth follows the same plot as most accounts of the mythic story. Pecola is abducted and raped and then undergoes a transformation of self that results in the creation of two distinct identities. Unlike Persephone who is physically kidnapped, Pecola's abduction is mental rather than physical. Pecola like many young Black girls becomes metaphorically abducted by the image of the white aesthetic. The opening pages of *The*

Bluest Eye intimate that Black girls' minds are abducted by primary school texts such as the Dick and Jane primer. . . .

In addition to introducing children to the Dick and Jane primer there are other subtle ways that the white aesthetic infiltrates Pecola's psyche. From candy wrappers, to movie stars and dolls Pecola cannot escape the culturally promoted image of blonde hair and blue eyes. As the narrator concedes bitterly: "the whole world had agreed that a blue-eyed, yellow-haired, pink-skinned doll was what every girl treasured. 'Here' they said, 'this is beautiful, and if you are on this day "worthy" you may have it'" (20–21). The narrator Claudia tries to resist the white aesthetic. Claudia dismembers the white dolls by breaking the fingers and pushing out the eyes. Later she treats her White playmates in the same violent manner.[8] Claudia, however, is no match for the hegemonic beauty myth defined by Naomi Wolf as "a currency system" and "a culturally imposed physical standard, which is an expression of power relations" (12) where men reign superior. Unfortunately, as Claudia matures she fails to maintain her repudiation of whiteness and learns to love the white dolls as much as Pecola does.

Without the money to purchase skin-bleaching creams or to access colored contact lenses that allow today's Black girls to buy into the fantasy of whiteness, Pecola must find other ways to make the transformation from Black to White. Pecola's resolve is to digest whiteness. She achieves this by eating Mary Jane candy (the candy wrapper features a blonde blue-eyed girl) and frequently drinking from a cup that is stamped with a picture of child icon Shirley Temple. Morrison shows that Pecola's fascination with whiteness is not unique. Pecola's foster sister, Frieda, is also enamored with Shirley Temple. Claudia recounts that both Pecola and Frieda would have loving conversations about how "cute Shirley Temple was" (19). Clearly these girls have been held hostage by the white aesthetic. With so many images of White female beauty, Black girls find it difficult to affirm their own beauty. . . .

After deconstructing the Dick and Jane myth Morrison turns her attention to reworking the Persephone and Demeter myth. Morrison's contemporary reworking of the Persephone and Demeter myth diverges from the Homeric and Ovidian narrative in significant ways. First, Morrison alters the sequence of the seasons. The *Homeric Hymn* opens in the springtime when the earth is fecund and the vegetation is ripe. Conversely, in the opening pages of *The Bluest Eye* the vibrant image of spring is replaced with the grayness of autumn. The narrator Claudia recalls the coldness of the autumn weather that brought on sickness and rough blankets. Morrison's change of seasonal cycles not only indicates the despondency of the characters, but the alteration is also "a sign that this text will turn upside down (the 'standard' archetype" (Hayes 174).

Morrison's rearrangement of the seasons illustrates that order in the universe has been disrupted. Demeter's separation from her daughter causes her to neglect the land and creates discord on the earth. Here, as in "In the Mecca," Morrison suggests that a steady diet of poverty, self-hatred, and oppression results in an environment that cannot foster life. Maureen Peal, who is described as the "disrupter of seasons" (62), reinforces the chaotic nature of the characters' lives. Maureen adds an uncharacteristic warmth to the winter imagery: "There was a hint of spring in her sloe green eyes, something summery in her complexion, and a rich autumn ripeness in her walk" (62). Maureen's association with spring and summer relate her to fertility and life. Her green eyes are representative of green plants budding in the spring and the "ripeness" of walk relates her to nature's harvest. Maureen possesses everything Pecola desires. She has fair skin, green eyes, and wealth. Although she is not White, she has light skin, which for Pecola is closer to White than she will ever be. Maureen is part of the idyllic White world that is juxtaposed against the painful Black world inhabited by Pecola and her friends. Throughout the narrative White and Black are transformed into binaries of the upper and lower world. The home of the Fishers for whom Pecola's mother works, for example, is emblematic of the utopian White world.[9] The flowers that frame the house symbolize life as well as beauty. In addition, not only the exterior of the house but also the interior décor is blindingly white. The Fisher home is antithetical to the description of Pecola's storefront, which is totally devoid of color, similar to the absence of color that occurs in the fall once the flowers begin wilting. Pecola, throughout the narrative remains locked in the darkness of her reality. It is only when she eats the Mary Jane candy or visits her mother at the Fisher home that she can step out of her darkness.

One of the most significant alterations to the archetypal myth is Morrison's reconfiguration of the death–rebirth motif. Each time Persephone descends into hell or ascends back to earth she experiences a death and rebirth of her identity. On earth Persephone is Demeter's daughter and in hell she is the bride of Hades. Because Pecola remains in hell she does not experience a transformation of self that coincides with the different spaces she inhabits. However, Pecola does experience an emotional death and rebirth. Each time she is demonized by schoolmates, parents, and members of the community she experiences a symbolic death of her Black identity as she rejects her Blackness and renews her wish for blue eyes. . . .

Pecola is literally born into a hellish existence. Her domestic environment is toxic and her parents perpetuate an attitude of internalized racism that teaches Pecola that like her parents she is ugly. The narrator informs us, "[T]heir ugliness was unique. No one could have convinced them that they were not relentlessly and aggressively ugly" (38). The Breedloves' ugliness consumes and defines them: "It was as though some mysterious all-knowing master had given each one a cloak of ugliness to wear, and they had each accepted it without question. The master had said, 'You are ugly people.' They had looked about themselves and saw nothing to contradict the statement, saw, in fact, support for it leaning at them from every billboard, every movie, every glance. . . . And they took the ugliness in their hands, threw it as a mantle over them, and went about the world with it" (39).

The Breedloves' physical ugliness manifests itself through violent "ugly" behavior. Pauline and Cholly constantly fight and Pecola is routinely beaten without cause, mentally assaulted, and later sexually molested. Pecola thinks if she were White with blue eyes life would be different, she would be loved: "It had occurred to Pecola some time ago that if her eyes, those eyes that held the pictures, and knew the sights—if those eyes of hers were different, that is to say beautiful, she would be different. . . . If she looked different, beautiful, maybe Cholly would be different, and Mrs. Breedlove too. Maybe they'd say, 'Why look at pretty-eyed Pecola. We mustn't do bad things in front of those pretty eyes'" (46).

In this instance it is clear that Pecola's desire for blue eyes is about more than being deemed attractive; rather, blue eyes would alleviate the chaos in her life and grant her the love and acceptance she craves.

The maternal bond between mother and daughter is integral to the Persephone–Demeter myth, especially the *Homeric Hymn*. . . . In the myth, Demeter's love for Persephone is unyielding. When Persephone is abducted her world is shattered; she does not eat or bathe. Likewise, while in hell Persephone grieves and also rejects food. In a major revision of Demeter and Persephone's relationship, Morrison presents a mother and daughter who are estranged. Pecola's detachment from Pauline is emphasized by her impersonal reference to Pauline as Ms. Breedlove. And where Demeter is personified as the ultimate nurturing and adoring mother, Pauline is cruel and abusive toward Pecola. . . . So when Pauline learns that Cholly rapes Pecola, unlike the mythic Demeter, Pauline is not overcome with grief. Instead, Pauline leaves Pecola in a situation where she can be, and is eventually, assaulted again. Moreover, Pecola becomes a victim twice. According to Collins many Black women who are raped suffer a dual victimization as they are abused first, by their rapist and then "are victimized again by family members, community residents, and social institutions" (147) who question their role in the rape. In Morrison's text, when Cholly impregnates Pecola, it is not Cholly but Pecola who is vilified by women in the community who suggest that Pecola encouraged the rape:

"Well they ought to take her out of school."
"Ought to. She carry some of the blame."
"Oh, come on. She ain't but twelve or so."
"Yeah. But you never know. How come she didn't fight him?"

"Maybe she did."
"Yeah? You never know." (189)

The function of the community in this text operates much the same way as the chorus in Greek tragedy. However, whereas traditionally the chorus serves as an objective commentator, the community stands in judgment of Pecola. Instead of the transition from death to life that Persephone experiences, Pecola remains in a cycle of death. With no Demeter character to save her, Pecola experiences repeated deaths that do not allow her to find liberation from her life in the underworld.

Pauline cannot protect Pecola from emotional abuse nor can she save her from the image of the white aesthetic because she, like Pecola, is also psychologically corrupted by the white aesthetic. The shared experiences of Pauline and Pecola once again links Morrison's narrative to the archetypal myth. In the ancient myth, Demeter, like her daughter, is also raped. In some accounts Poseidon rapes her and in other versions she claims pirates rape her. Also, in ancient art and literature Persephone's and Demeter's identities are often merged into one identity. The two women's similar experiences of loss and their subsequent transformations present them as "separate-yet-one" (Carlson 23). In *The Bluest Eye*, Pecola relives her mother's experiences. As a young girl, Pauline, like Pecola feels alienated by members of the community. Pauline's Southern mannerisms, her inability to dress as well as other women, and her failure to apply cosmetics tastefully leave her open for ridicule. Pauline is hurt by the women's "goading glances and private snickers at her way of talking (saying 'chil'ren')" (188). Similar to Pecola's fascination with Shirley Temple, Pauline finds her salvation in the movie theater where she escapes to the fantasy of the White world. At the movies she learns to "assign" faces to categories "of absolute beauty" (122), with White faces, like actress Jean Harlow's, occupying the top of the scale."[10] When Pauline secures a job as a domestic she is able finally to leave behind the ugliness and Blackness of her own underworld reality and enter the Dick and Jane world. Pauline desires so much to become part of the order and normalcy of this White world that she neglects her own household as well as her own children in favor of her White charge. Pauline's surrogate motherhood is another play on the mythic theme. After Persephone has been abducted, Demeter becomes a nursemaid for Demophoön. Demophoön offers Demeter the ability to serve as a surrogate mother and subdue her grief. In an effort to make Demophoön immortal, "at night she would bury him like a brand in the fire's might" (qtd. Foley 14). In Morrison's novel Pauline cannot immortalize her charge, but she is able to rear this symbolic Shirley Temple figure as if she were her own daughter.

Notes

8. Donald Gibson suggests that Claudia's attempt to dismember the dolls is also an attempt to dismember the myth of White beauty. Gibson, "Text and Countertext in Toni Morrison's *The Bluest Eye*," *Literature, Interpretation, Theory* 1 (1989): 21.

9. The Fishers give Pauline a sense of self-worth.

10. A similar idea is featured in *Maud Martha*.

Works by Toni Morrison

NOVELS

The Bluest Eye, 1970.

Sula, 1973.

Song of Solomon, 1977.

Tar Baby, 1981.

Beloved, 1987.

Jazz, 1992.

Paradise, 1998.

Love, 2003.

A Mercy, 2007.

NONFICTION

The Black Book, 1974.

Playing in the Dark: Whiteness and the Literary Imagination, 1992.

Race-ing Justice, En-gendering Power: Essays on Anita Hill, Clarence Thomas, and the Construction of Social Reality, editor, 1992.

Birth of a Nation'hood: Gaze, Script, and Spectacle in the O.J. Simpson Case, coeditor, 1997.

Remember: The Journey to School Integration, 2004.

What Moves at the Margin: Selected Nonfiction, 2008.

PLAYS AND LIBRETTI

Dreaming Emmett, first performed in 1986.

Margaret Garner, first performed in 2005.

Annotated Bibliography

Christian, Barbara. *Black Women Novelists: The Development of a Tradition, 1892–1976.* Westport, Conn., and London: Greenwood Press, 1980.

This study of black women writers looks back from the decade of the 1970s, when the idea of black women writing was beginning to get the attention it deserved. At the time there were several black women writers whose works were unpublished, even unknown, but, according to the author, the antecedents of the great works we have today were clearly present in them. The author examines these writers and texts and concludes with chapters on three accomplished black women writers—Toni Morrison, Paule Marshall, and Alice Walker—who have built on the efforts of those who struggled unrecognized before them.

Conner, Marc C., ed. *The Aesthetics of Toni Morrison: Speaking the Unspeakable.* Jackson: University Press of Mississippi, 2000.

This volume of essays addresses a perceived gap in the literary criticism of Toni Morrison's novels. According to Conner, there has been an emphasis on the specifically African and African-American sources for her writing at the expense of ignoring Morrison's substantial education in the classic Western writers, including the great Greek playwrights. Morrison, for example, wrote her master's thesis on the works of William Faulkner and Virginia Woolf, using insights from Greek tragedy. The essays include focus on the more aesthetic features of Morrison's art, looking at theories of the sublime, the beautiful, and the mysterious for a new perspective on her writing.

Feng, Pin-chia. *The Female* Bildungsroman *by Toni Morrison and Maxine Hong Kingston: A Postmodern Reading.* New York: Peter Lang Publishing, Inc., 1998.

Feng divides her focus on two novels by Morrison, *The Bluest Eye* and *Sula*, and two by Kingston, *The Woman Warrior* and *China Men*. Feng explains in her first chapter that she is drawing on resources more commonly associated with women—namely, repressed memory, which she refers to as "the politics of rememory"—to expand the traditionally male genre of bildungsroman, a coming-of-age narrative in which a young (usually male) protagonist establishes his identity through undergoing a form of heroic quest. Her discussions of *The Bluest Eye* focus on the two girls—Pecola and Claudia—who, despite being of the same sex and race and from the same community, confront the challenge of their circumstances with very different outcomes.

Fultz, Lucille P. *Toni Morrison: Playing with Difference*. Urbana and Chicago: University of Illinois Press, 2003.

Toni Morrison is a self-reflexive and self-conscious writer who encourages her readers to participate in the evolution of meaning and form in her work. Lucille P. Fultz traces this evolution and analyzes the devices Morrison uses to engage the reader. One of these technical devices is the use of multiple perspectives, in which the reader is asked to suspend judgment until all the viewpoints have been presented.

Gates, Henry Louis, Jr., and K.A. Appiah, eds. *Toni Morrison: Critical Perspectives Past and Present*. New York: Amistad Press, Inc., 1993.

Declaring that Toni Morrison is the most (or among the most) "formally sophisticated novelist in the history of African-American literature," Henry Louis Gates Jr. has assembled a lengthy and broad collection of commentary on the author. The book is divided into three sections—reviews, essays, and interviews with the author. The novels covered include *The Bluest Eye*, *Sula*, *Song of Solomon*, *Tar Baby*, *Beloved*, and *Jazz*. A chronology of Morrison's life and a lengthy bibliography are also included.

Harris, Trudier. *Fiction and Folklore: The Novels of Toni Morrison*. Knoxville: University of Tennessee Press, 1991.

In the introductory comments, Harris reminds the reader that as late as the 1830s it was illegal to teach slaves to read and for this reason transmission of information and wisdom deemed essential for the education of black people relied on oral tradition. Harris argues that this element of folklore is fundamental to all African-American literature and that Toni Morrison explicitly and deliberately uses features of oral tradition to engage the reader in the visceral experience of her characters' lives. Within this framework, five of her novels—*The Bluest Eye, Sula, Song of Solomon, Tar Baby,* and *Beloved*—are discussed. Harris discusses *The Bluest Eye* as the novel that relies most extensively on elements of oral tradition.

Holloway, Karla F.C., and Stephanie A. Demetrakopoulos. *New Dimensions of Spirituality: A Biracial and Bicultural Reading of the Novels of Toni Morrison.* New York, Westport, Conn., and London: Greenwood Press, 1987.

This study of Morrison's novels is distinctive for being written by two women who include in their commentary views on the other's reading of text. In their introduction, Holloway and Demetrakopoulos present their differences in background, literary training, and culture; one is white, the other black; one is mainly focused on black studies and language, the other on women's studies and Jungian psychology. Initially they had intended to write a series of chapters on each of Morrison's novels, but they noticed as they proceeded how their commentary was reflecting significant differences in the way they heard and understood Morrison's words. That discovery— and further analysis of what these differences mean and why they matter—became an additional element of their book. Each author comments on Morrison's novels from *The Bluest Eye* to *Tar Baby,* addressing other topics, such as racial memory and Morrison's contributions to culture as well.

King, Lovalerie, and Lynne Orilla Scott, eds. *James Baldwin and Toni Morrison: Comparative Critical and Theoretical Essays.* New York: Palgrave Macmillan, 2006.

This collection of essays brings together the work of Toni Morrison and James Baldwin—two writers generally regarded as the most significant figures in twentieth-century African-American literature. The introductory chapter explains the extent and nature of the Morrison-Baldwin personal relationship, which began in the 1970s when Morrison was working as an editor at Random House. Their friendship lasted until Baldwin's death in the late 1980s. Both writers appreciatively read and commented on each other's writing and made several public statements indicating their mutual admiration and indebtedness.

Mayberry, Susan Neal. *Can't I Love What I Criticize?: The Masculine and Morrison*. Athens and London: The University of Georgia Press, 2007.

Toni Morrison's views on feminist issues cannot be easily categorized. In this study of Morrison and masculinity, Mayberry begins where Morrison does—discussing a brand of feminism in black culture that cannot be defined without including the masculine perspective. With this point established, she analyzes Morrison's novels from *The Bluest* Eye (1970) to *Love* (2003).

Mbalia, Doreatha Drummond. *Toni Morrison's Developing Class Consciousness*, 2nd edition. Selinsgrove, Penn.: Susquehanna University Press, 2004.

In her preface to the first edition, Mbalia explains that she was moved to discuss and analyze Morrison after she noticed an evolution in her work that demonstrated her commitment to writing as a way to help African Americans confront and resolve the dilemmas they have historically faced and continue to face. She explains in the preface to the second edition that she has added three chapters—one each on *Jazz* and *Paradise* and one titled "A Praisesong for Toni Morrison, A Call to Action for Her Readers." A second section on Morrison's use of her own life experiences in her writing is another addition.

McKay, Nellie Y., and Kathryn Earle, eds. *Approaches to Teaching the Novels of Toni Morrison*. New York: The Modern Language Association of America, 1997.

This title is one of many in the *Approaches to Teaching* series. Although written for teachers, the several essays in the collection present the novels of Toni Morrison from such diverse perspectives that they are valuable for a range of readers. One essay, for example, deals with the special issues that potentially arise when discussing the scene of a black man raping his daughter in a class with male black students. Another essay deals with issues raised about class and class consciousness.

Middleton, David L., ed. *Toni Morrison's Fiction: Contemporary Criticism*. New York and London: Garland Publishing, Inc., 2000.

This collection of essays was assembled after Toni Morrison had been awarded the Nobel Prize and is based on the assumption that a permanent place has been established for her work in the American canon. Much critical analysis of Morrison's work has already been published, and the essays in this volume discuss some of this earlier commentary in order to expand appreciation for the range of her accomplishments. Specifically, the essays are considerations of the connections between her work and that of other cultures. Morrison's novels in order of publication through *Jazz* are considered.

Schreiber, Evelyn Jaffe. *Subversive Voices: Eroticizing the Other in William Faulkner and Toni Morrison*. Knoxville: University of Tennessee Press, 2001.

Schreiber explains in her preface how she began as an admiring reader and scholar of the works of William Faulkner and was fascinated to discover how similar she found her later experience of reading the works of Toni Morrison, especially *Beloved*. This book brings together observations of the similarities between these writers and their important differences. Schreiber's main focus is each writer's treatment of characters living on the margins of mainstream society.

Taylor-Guthrie, Danille, ed. *Conversations with Toni Morrison*. Jackson: University Press of Mississippi, 1994.

This volume gathers the most memorable interviews Toni Morrison gave from 1974 to 1992. Some are mainly academic, discussing her developing themes and style, as well as her influences; others are transcripts from television interviews, including one with Bill Moyers. Most contain some commentary about *The Bluest Eye* and its extensive impact on her career and evolution as a writer.

Walters, Tracey L. *African American Literature and the Classicist Tradition: Black Women Writers from Wheatley to Morrison.* New York: Palgrave Macmillan, 2007.

This seminal study looks at the ingenious ways that African-American women writers have made use of Western classical myth and tradition in their own writing. African-American women have had to contend with a disproportionate amount of oppression, discrimination, and prejudice and have suffered, sometimes silently, egregious abuse. The classical tradition is known for its engagement of the extremes of pain and hardship—"speaking the unspeakable"—an element that many black women writers have found helpful in conveying their observations and experiences. Another recurring theme in classical myth—that of the mother figure and the mother/daughter pair—has been useful in conveying truths about family life and relationships between generations.

Williams, Lisa. *The Artist as Outsider in the Novels of Toni Morrison and Virginia Woolf.* Westport, Conn., and London: Greenwood Press, 2000.

Reading this study of Morrison and Woolf would require substantial familiarity with the work of both authors. Williams takes a fascinating look at the ways both women dealt with the artist figure in society and the experience of being artists themselves in very different cultural settings and historical times. Williams points out that Woolf was consciously striving to describe and create the difficult and necessary isolation women writers find themselves in, and her readership was understood to be white educated women. Race is not an issue in her writings. Morrison, by contrast, having frequently been the only black person in her classes during her early school years and, later, as a professor teaching in mainly white universities the works of mainly white male writers had an extra level of isolation to deal with. Yet Morrison also knew—as Woolf had not—the experience of a nourishing family and female cultural production and subjectivity. Williams points out that these two women, coming from sharply different perspectives, showed in their writing the destructive consequences of internalizing "whiteness" and "class."

Contributors

Harold Bloom is Sterling Professor of the Humanities at Yale University. He is the author of 30 books, including *Shelley's Mythmaking, The Visionary Company, Blake's Apocalypse, Yeats, A Map of Misreading, Kabbalah and Criticism, Agon: Toward a Theory of Revisionism, The American Religion, The Western Canon,* and *Omens of Millennium: The Gnosis of Angels, Dreams, and Resurrection. The Anxiety of Influence* sets forth Professor Bloom's provocative theory of the literary relationships between the great writers and their predecessors. His most recent books include *Shakespeare: The Invention of the Human,* a 1998 National Book Award finalist, *How to Read and Why, Genius: A Mosaic of One Hundred Exemplary Creative Minds, Hamlet: Poem Unlimited, Where Shall Wisdom Be Found?,* and *Jesus and Yahweh: The Names Divine.* In 1999, Professor Bloom received the prestigious American Academy of Arts and Letters Gold Medal for Criticism. He has also received the International Prize of Catalonia, the Alfonso Reyes Prize of Mexico, and the Hans Christian Andersen Bicentennial Prize of Denmark.

Stephanie A. Demetrakopoulos has been a professor of English at Western Michigan University. She is the author of *Listening to Our Bodies: The Rebirth of Feminine Wisdom* and helped compile *Black American Feminisms: A Multidisciplinary Bibliography.* She has contributed essays on feminism and literature to several publications, including the journal *Trivia: Voices of Feminism.*

Trudier Harris is a professor of English at the University of North Carolina at Chapel Hill, where she teaches African-American literature and folklore to undergraduates and graduate students. In addition to more than 20 authored or edited volumes, Harris published a memoir, *Summer Snow: Reflections from a Black Daughter of the South* (2003). She has received several awards for excellence in teaching, including the Governor's Award for Excellence in Teaching in 2005.

120

Marc C. Conner teaches in the English department at Washington and Lee University. In addition to his work on Toni Morrison, Conner has published essays on Sherwood Anderson, Thomas Pynchon, and Salman Rushdie. His recent scholarly interests center on the presence of the sublime and the beautiful in twentieth-century American literature.

Lisa Williams teaches writing, literature, and women's studies in the English department at Ramapo College of New Jersey. She has published essays in *Women's Studies Quarterly, Virginia Woolf Miscellany*, and *Transformations: A Resource for Curriculum Transformation and Scholarship*. In response to the 2001 attack on the World Trade Center and the subsequent U.S. military response, Williams wrote *Letters to Virginia Woolf*, explaining that of the several writers she was familiar with, Woolf had expressed antiwar views that were of particular relevance to the new global situation.

Evelyn Jaffe Schreiber teaches English at George Washington University and is director of the Writing Center there. Her academic interests focus on applying the theories of Jacques Lacan to issues of subjectivity and race.

Lucille P. Fultz teaches English at Rice University, specializing in African-American literature and culture. She has published several articles on Toni Morrison and, in 1991, co-edited *Double Stitch: Black Women Write About Mothers and Daughters*.

Doreatha Drummond Mbalia teaches in the Department of Africology at the University of Wisconsin at Milwaukee. Her interests include pan-Africanism, African women's studies, and Africa and the diaspora.

Lynne Orilla Scott has been a visiting assistant professor at James Madison College at Michigan State University. In addition to several essays and articles on African-American literature, Scott published *James Baldwin's Later Fiction: Witness*

121

to the Journey in 2002 and wrote about Baldwin in the *African American Review* in 2004.

Susan Neal Mayberry has, in addition to her work on Morrison, written critical essays on Tennessee Williams and Richard Wright. She is a contributor to the *African American Review*.

Tracey L. Walters teaches literature at Stony Brook University. She has written extensively about black female writers and specifically about classical myth in African-American literature.

Acknowledgments

Stephanie A. Demetrakopoulos, "Bleak Beginnings: *The Bluest Eye*." From *New Dimensions of Spirituality: A Biracial and Bicultural Reading of the Novels of Toni Morrison*, pp. 31–33, 35–36. Published by Greenwood Press. Copyright © 1987 by Karla F. C. Holloway and Stephanie A. Demetrakopoulos. Reproduced with permission of ABC-CLIO, LLC.

Trudier Harris, "*The Bluest Eye*: A Wasteland in Lorain, Ohio." From *Fiction and Folklore: The Novels of Toni Morrison*, pp. 27–31, 196–197. Published by the University of Tennessee Press. Copyright © 1991 by Trudier Harris.

Marc C. Conner, "From the Sublime to the Beautiful: The Aesthetic Progression of Toni Morrison." From *The Aesthetics of Toni Morrison: Speaking the Unspeakable*, pp. 49–50, 52–55, 74–76. Copyright © 2000 by and reproduced with the permission of the University Press of Mississippi.

Lisa Williams, "*The Bluest Eye*." From *The Artist as Outsider in the Novels of Toni Morrison and Virginia Woolf*, pp. 53, 55–56, 58, 62–64, 70–74. Published by Greenwood Press. Copyright © 2000 by Lisa Williams.

Evelyn Jaffe Schreiber, "Identity Formation: The Double-Voiced Text of *The Bluest Eye*." From *Subversive Voices: Eroticizing the Other in William Faulkner and Toni Morrison*, pp. 77–78, 80–84, 93–94, 164–165. Copyright © 2001 by the University of Tennessee Press.

Lucille P. Fultz, "Narrating the Pain of Difference." From *Toni Morrison: Playing with Difference*, pp. 50–53, 116–117. Published by University of Illinois Press. Copyright © 2003 by the Board of Trustees of the University of Illinois.

Doreatha Drummond Mbalia, "*The Bluest Eye*: The Need for Racial Approbation." From *Toni Morrison's Developing Class Consciousness*, pp. 32–37, 217–219. Published by Susquehanna University Press. Copyright © 1991 by Associated University Presses, Inc. and © 2004 by Rosemont Publishing & Printing.

Lynn Orilla Scott, "Revising the Incest Story." From *James Baldwin and Toni Morrison: Comparative Critical and Theoretical Essays*, edited by Lovalerie King and Lynn Orilla Scott, pp. 87–90, 98–101. Copyright © 2006 by Lovalerie King and Lynn Orilla Scott. Reproduced with permission of Palgrave Macmillan.

Susan Neal Mayberry, "Black Boys, White Gaze: Publication of *The Bluest Eye*." From *Can't I Love What I Criticize: The Masculine and Morrison*, pp. 30–32, 299–301. Copyright © 2007 by the University of Georgia Press.

Tracey L. Walters, "The Destruction and Reconstruction of Myth in Morrison: The Persephone Myth in *The Bluest Eye*." From *African American Literature and the Classicist Tradition: Black Women Writers from Wheatley to Morrison*, pp. 112–114, 116–124, 179–180. Copyright © Tracey L. Walters, 2007. Reproduced with permission of Palgrave Macmillan.

Index